FINISH STRONG:
THE DAN RUSSELL STORY

FINISH STRONG

THE DAN RUSSELL STORY

by **DAN RUSSELL**
with CRAIG BORLASE

Finish Strong: The Dan Russell Story
Published by **Rising Star Studios**, LLC. Edina, Minnesota.

Copyright © 2015 Finish Strong LLC.

ISBN 978-1-936770-70-0

The accounts in this book are true to the author's recollection and used with permission of the primary individuals involved.

Book layout and cover design by Phillip Walton.
Photographs by Joel Davis.

Second Edition
Printed in China

CONTENTS

THE UNOFFICIAL CHAMPION OF THE WORLD

I was wearing a rubber suit, woolen hat, and gloves. On top of the suit was a sweatshirt and sweatpants, and on top of them were more sweatshirts and sweatpants. Barely able to breathe, I was riding an exercise bike, which I had placed in a sauna somewhere in the middle of a city a thousand miles east of Moscow. And this was all perfectly normal. In fact, it was essential. Not only was it helping me to sweat out the last twelve pounds that were going to get me to my desired weight, but the sweat, the pain, and the way my breath threatened to rip my lungs out from my chest with every agonizing inhalation was just what I needed. I was a wrestler. Pain and discipline were my two best friends.

I hadn't always embraced pain. There had been times when, as a younger child barely into puberty, the punishing starvation regimes were too much for me. I hadn't learned to channel that dizzying, hollow feeling into something that could help me on the mat. Instead, I let it get the better of me. I used to worry about food being scarce, and there were nights when the house was asleep that I'd sneak down to the refrigerator and allow myself to take one thing from the fridge.

Most times on these secret raids I'd pick a leftover from the meal I'd been a spectator at just a few hours before. A slice of cake. A handful of meatloaf. But I wouldn't gorge on it. I wouldn't even lick off any food that happened to get stuck on my fingers. With all the precision and care of a surgeon, I'd remove the item from the shelf, carefully guiding my hands by the clinical light. I'd take the food and wrap it in the foil I'd placed ready on the counter. My mouth would be salivating like crazy by this point, but I wouldn't let it distract me. Once wrapped tightly, I'd take my prize back up to my room and place it at the top of my wardrobe, next to all the other creased silver blocks that were stacking up like bricks. Other boys my age hid porn, alcohol, or cigarettes away from their parents' gaze. I hid mac and cheese. Knowing it was close to me made me feel safe.

But all that was behind me by the time I perfected the art of losing seven percent of my total body weight within two hours by sweating myself to the point of near-total dehydration. I had learned that the battle that was fought on the mat was nothing compared to the battle fought within me. I had learned to embrace the pain that came from hunger, to allow it to sharpen my mind. When I cut weight my mind became focused, turning me from a shotgun into a rifle. When I pushed myself through pain, I became a warrior, the very wrestler that my father had envisaged when I was a small boy.

And on the day I was in the Russian sauna, I needed my routine more than ever. I pedaled like fury for fifteen minutes before resting on the bike for a further fifteen then stepped outside for five before starting it all over again. As my breathing tore at my chest I knew I was raging through the battle like never before. For months I had been working for this, starving myself even more than usual to drop the forty pounds I needed to lose to be able to compete in my ideal weight class. I had been training a minimum of four hours a day, six days a week and I was leaner, stronger, and more focused than at any point in my life. I'd had multiple knee surgeries, been concussed more times than was good for me and had even recovered from a broken back three years earlier. I was twenty-seven years old, in the peak of physical condition and my lifetime's goal was just waiting for me to grab it. There was not one doubt in my mind that I was just twelve months away from becoming the Olympic champion.

Dan Russell sweating off weight before a match.

Russia's Poddubny Championship was key to making this happen. If the Olympics are like a symphony orchestra recital – polished and perfect, then Poddubny is like Springsteen – a raucous celebration for true connoisseurs of the art. It's the top of the tree, a challenge unlike any other, an unofficial world championship that takes place each year in a different Russian location. And only one American had ever won there before.

I'd competed at the previous Poddubny Championship in 1990, and it hadn't started too well for me. My first match had been against the reigning world champion – a Russian who had two Olympic medals and three world medals behind him. I had a game plan that was about as sophisticated and mature as a playground scrap, built around the single hope that I would somehow get lucky. I didn't. He schooled me.

That first match in my first Poddubny had taught me that luck is for gamblers, not fighters. But it brought into focus so many other lessons that I had been learning since I was five. It reminded me that a wrestler must dig in, wrestle toe-to-toe, be prepared to grapple with the fight – to embrace it, not hope for a lucky escape. A wrestler must be in the moment, constantly present, never letting his attention wander. A wrestler must always go forward, never backward. A wrestler always pushes, never pauses. A wrestler must finish strong.

Nothing about Greco-Roman wrestling is easy. There are no short cuts and there are no quick fixes. There is nothing to hide behind – no equipment that could

fail you, no teammates to put the blame on. There's
not even a jersey you can bury your head in. It's just
you, on a brightly lit mat, in a skin-tight singlet trying
to win. You cannot hide your fear and you cannot hide
your lack of preparation. You cannot hide your weaknesses and you cannot hide your tactics. Everything is
on display out there.

It's the way that Greco-Roman wrestling has always
been. Since 708 BC when it was introduced into the
ancient Olympic Games, all the way through to Athens
in 1896 when it was at the heart of the first of the
Modern Olympic Games, Greco-Roman has been one of
the ultimate tests of one-on-one combat. It's wrestling
from the waist up, which means you can't grab or trip
your opponent's legs. The aim is to pin your opponent's
shoulders to the mat, but how you get them down there
on the ground is where the magic happens. Greco-
Roman is all about the throws, so the higher and harder
you launch someone the more you are rewarded. It's an
explosive sport, and a dangerous one too. Power matters, but a good technique can see a tall, lanky guy like I
was throw a chiseled stack of Russian muscle down like
a rag doll.

At least, that's what I was hoping as I stepped out of
the bus outside the auditorium for the weigh-in for the
1995 Poddubny Championship in Perm, Russia. It was
February and the city was in the middle of a prolonged
and savage winter. For fifty-two days the temperature
refused to rise above zero degrees Fahrenheit, and on
the coldest days the mercury had sunk as low as -28.
The air stung as you inhaled and each joint ached with

the cold. Added to that, thanks to my time in the sauna the day before, I was severely dehydrated and trying carefully to replenish my supplies without causing my body any problems.

You see, the trouble with sweating off so much weight so quickly is that your body craves water and will do anything to retain it. If you give in to the urge to gulp down a few liters as soon as the weigh-in is over you can end up bloated and puffy, with swollen joints and limbs that have lost all their speed and power. So, having tortured your body in the sauna, you have to torture it some more.

I walked past the soot-colored snow that was piled up outside the gray concrete building, sipping the air like I sipped the water. I liked the fact that the cold air added to the pain of weight loss. It made me feel alert and hungry and ready to focus on every moment of the battle ahead.

There must have been two, maybe three hundred wrestlers in the hall for the weigh-in. Apart from the shiny new Soviet decor that looked as though it had been perfectly preserved from the 1950s, the scene was the same as any other wrestling tournament you could go into today. Wrestlers come in all shapes and sizes, from fat-free five-footers, bursting with energy and fizz, to supersized heavyweights who lumber like giant bears at the zoo. Out of the seven weight categories, the biggest single number of wrestlers belonged to mine – the 163 pounders. It's a weight that represents the greatest number of wrestlers, and it holds the greatest range of body types. There are the shorter, explosive ones as well as the bigger ones with more power. And then there are the people like me – lanky, not too much going on with the muscles, but aiming to leverage those long limbs to lift and throw whoever's in front of us.

I was looking at my opponents lining up before the scales. I'd traveled widely by this time and knew Russian wrestlers weren't always as heavy as they appeared. With their chiseled jaws and perfectly defined muscles I sometimes wondered whether they had hollow bones. But I reminded myself that appearances can be deceptive: even though the guys with muscles stacked on muscles look mean and threatening, those big, explosive muscles get tired throughout the match's five minute bouts.

Still, I was a little bothered when Anatoly, my coach, dug his finger into my ribs and growled at me in his thick Russian accent, "Why you wrestle at one six three? You too small for this. You should lose more weight and drop down to be with your own kind."

Drop more weight? You've gotta love that gray, negative Soviet outlook on life. Anatoly had been my coach for years and I'd grown to love his Russian ways – the lack of praise, the dissatisfaction with anything but the best, the way everything on his face pointed downward whenever he was talking, thinking, or just walking about the wrestling room. I'd grown to hear his voice and his voice only in my head. But drop yet more weight? That was never going to happen.

The hall was packed. Wrestling in the US is nothing like wrestling in Russia, throughout the former Soviet Union or the Middle East. For the most part our tournament crowds rattle around school gyms, too much space between them as the sound echoes off the walls. But not overseas. There the crowds can be colossal, with wrestlers treated as rock stars and tournaments uniting the whole city in celebration. Perm was just like that. There were artists and singers gathered from across the region, all heavily expectant of boosting their national pride as their countrymen took on the handful of wrestlers from the rest of the world.

"Who's my first fight?" I asked Anatoly as he flicked through the thick sheets of the tournament schedule.

"Sayenko," he said. "Local boy. You must be ready."

I didn't need to be told twice and set off to warm up. That final hour before the first fight of a competition can be the toughest to get through. Once more you have to force your body to sweat, this time getting rid of any traces of swelling that have settled in your joints despite holding back on the water intake.

An hour later and I was on the mat. I always loved the noise these crowds made, especially when there was a local boy fighting. There were only ten of us from the US competing, and we all knew the crowds wanted nothing better than to see us get whopped in front of their eyes. I couldn't blame them, but by the time I reached my hand out to greet Sayenko, the only thing I was aware of was the fight ahead of me.

The whistle blew and I went at him with all I had.
Right away I could tell he was not just some local club
wrestler who'd gotten lucky. He was a serious fighter –
lanky but sculpted – and the challenge was way more
than I had expected. Every second required my full
attention and focus and I knew one mistake could cost
me the whole match. So I pushed. I pulled. I did not let
my concentration falter. And as the buzzer announced
that the round was over, I looked to the scoreboard. I
had won the match three to two.

The crowd was momentarily stunned. Then, as I
stepped down from the stage, they ignited. It was a
little overwhelming at first, all those people crowding
around, the younger ones wanting my autograph, the
older ones reaching out to shake my hand. There was
no animosity, just appreciation and respect. And just
as with every victory, Anatoly's face lost the intensely
focused expression and radiated nothing but joy. "Good
job," he drawled. "You fight like a Russian."

I was taken by the security guards into a side room,
where a handful of journalists were waiting to ask
me some questions. How had I reacted when I knew
I was fighting Sayenko first of all? Did I know he had
won the tournament that had determined the Russian
National Team – a tournament that had earned him a
brand new car and a big old lump of rubles? Did I think
that I would now go on and win the whole Poddubny
tournament?

One match does not make a champion, and I knew
there were more battles ahead. I wasn't going to let

fantasy or wishful thinking keep me from engaging in the fight, yet I felt good all the way through the next matches, staying present in every single one as I moved into the second day of the tournament. And as so often happens, when I embraced the battle, the winning took care of itself.

With just four undefeated wrestlers left in my weight category, I was beginning to get used to seeing Anatoly's half smile sneaking back at me. But the moment he came back with news of my semi-final opponent, his face had lost all traces of joy and pride. "Eest no good," he said; I was up against Chagiev, a Russian I knew well from my time back at the Olympic Training Center in Colorado Springs. I'd never fought him, but we regularly studied the best wrestlers from around the world, looking for examples of great technique. Chagiev was a regular on our VCR.

Fear has a way of creeping in through the smallest of cracks, and Anatoly had just blown a hole large enough for a whole torrent of self-doubt to flood into my mind. Standing by the stage, waiting for my name to be called up for the match, I felt the temptation to give in to fear. Flashbacks of the humiliation of losing so badly at the last Poddubny dominated my thoughts, but I forced my mind to focus on the right things instead. It did not matter who I had to face. I would have to scrap for every point. I reminded myself of my training. I could not have been better prepared. Had I given 100% in the build up to the tournament? *Yes, I had.* Was I prepared to give 100%, to embrace the fight? *Yes, I was.* Was I ready to let winning take care of itself? "Yes!" I shouted, loud enough to interrupt the announcer and make a few people stare. But I didn't care. I was ready for the battle. I wiped the bottom of my shoes on the edge of the mat like a bull ready to charge. My eyes were narrowed, my arms swinging. I stepped onto the stage with all the confidence I could muster. There was Chagiev, short and stocky with the kind of mustache that only a real man could grow. We shook hands and got ready to fight.

I charged forward the moment I heard the whistle. I drove him right off the mat. It's a great tactic when you're facing an aggressive wrestler – take control from the start, get them on defense, refuse to allow them to get their offensive plan into play. A winning wrestler is most often the one who controls the pace and rhythm of the match, plus, the rules are clear: whoever goes off the mat first gets a caution and point against him and the match restarts with the aggressive wrestler on top as the passive one crouches on all fours. Chagiev and I hustled back to the center of the ring, me thinking I was one point up and about to be able to get behind my opponent and give him my gut wrench. I've always liked my gut wrench, especially when you can feel your opponent's ribs really start to give way under the pressure. But none of the three officials indicated they thought I had scored, so the referee called "No points!" and I went back to facing Chagiev.

Whenever you're overseas and wrestling an opponent in their homeland you always figure you are three points down before the match even starts. It's just the way home field advantage goes. You can't worry about calls that go against you, and you have to accept that anything controversial is never going to go your way – especially when you are wearing an American singlet. You just have to take it, forget trying to whine to the officials, and stay present in the fight. You're not there to make the calls; you're there to wrestle.

I drove Chagiev off the mat for a second time, ran back to the center and stole a glance at the officials as if to say, "You have to call it right this time!" They looked back, faces stone cold. "No points," declared the referee.

Right then was when I knew there was no way that they were going to let me beat Chagiev in Russia, so there was no point at all in my trying to win over the officials. The only battle that mattered was the one on the mat. I would have to scrap for every hold and every twist. I would not let myself stop fighting even for the tiniest fraction of a second. I upped my intensity even more, always moving, bouncing, not letting him settle into any kind of rhythm. Chagiev was four inches shorter than me and so I kept on pulling down on his head. After several minutes of my heavy hands tugging at his neck like a bear, I knew he'd get frustrated, maybe even start to worry that I'd be doing him some damage. I got him into a front headlock, scored a takedown, then gut wrenched him and locked like a python around his ribcage, squeezing and then turning him to expose his back. Three points. He gut wrenched me for two, and as the match progressed, I knew he was going to get even more dangerous. Chagiev was going to come at me like a hurricane and with any mistake I made – if I allowed my elbow to come even a few inches away from my body – he would explode into me and send me flying.

With ten seconds to go I was winning three to two. My game plan was working, though I knew that even with so little time left I had to keep my focus sharp. I have seen too many matches lost in the final seconds as one wrestler relaxes, thinking the bout is his. So I expected Chagiev to come at me hard as we tussled in the center of the ring with eight seconds left. But instead he pushed out at me, both hands hard on my chest, growling something I didn't understand before turning around and walking right out of the gym. It was awesome. Chagiev, the famous Greco-Roman super-star, quit in Russia, in front of all those Russian fans, all those Russian officials. I'd never seen a world-class wrestler quit during a match like that before, and the whole building seemed to be just as shocked. Yet again the room was silent, but once the noise started up it took a while for the commotion to settle down. But in time my arm was raised. I had just one match left for the title. One more match for gold.

I couldn't wait for the final, but time slowed as the afternoon leaked into the evening. Once I had cooled down from the Chagiev match I started my inner dia-logue, the same routine I always went through. Had I given my all in training? Yes. Was I prepared to give everything in the match? Yes. Was I prepared to let win-ning take care of itself? "Yes!" I shouted again. Even if the whole hall had stopped and stared at me, I wouldn't have noticed. I was in my zone. Nothing else mattered.

I knew I would need to be at my best. My opponent was a guy named Totlak, another Russian. All through the tournament as my teammates and I had wandered around the arena, watching the matches in progress, I'd drawn their attention to the one wrestler who stood out from them all. Short and stocky, he was insanely powerful with a beautiful technique. We had all stared as he threw one opponent with such force that he had to be stretchered away to the local hospital. "See that guy?" I'd said. "To win my weight class I have to get through him."

Standing on the mat, Totlak and I on each side of the referee, the announcer went on and on with his introductions. I had no way of being able to understand exactly what it was he was saying, but I guessed he was listing all of Totlak's many achievements. As the speech went on Anatoly started to yell my name and call me over to join him at the corner. He sounded like he was desperate to talk so I ran to his side.

I hoped he was going to give me some last-minute advice that would make all the difference, like "Lead with your left foot, Russell," or "Get on that two-one-one and don't let go." Instead his eyes locked on to mine and he said, as if both our lives depended on it, "Dan, the medal is solid gold, worth five thousand dollars MINIMUM. You must win!" And with that, he pushed me hard back to the center of the mat.

It took me a second to get my head back, just in time to see Totlak staring back at me with the kind of look that all champion wrestlers have before a fight: hungry,

Coach Anatoly Petrosyan still going strong in 2015

impatient, alive. My mind began to race and momentarily presented me with an image of myself being driven down onto the mat, head first. I dragged my mind back with the words that I had said a hundred times already during the previous days. Fight the fear! Get focused! Love the fight! Embrace the battle! I inhaled deeply. I narrowed my focus. I was ready. We shook hands. The whistle blew. The biggest match of my life began.

It's a terrible feeling when someone has you in a front headlock – your head forced down so your chin is on your chest and the back of your skull is being pulled hard into your opponent's belly. It's hard to breathe down there, but it's the fear of what's coming next that really gets most people. If your opponent can move his legs just right, if he has proper technique, then he can turn your chin to one side, lean back, throw his hips in and pull up on your twisted head and throat. The pressure on your neck will be immense, and there will come a point where your body's survival instincts will take over rather than letting you risk dislocating your vertebrae. That's when your body will allow itself to be thrown, your feet tracing a wide arc as they sail through the air, every muscle in your back preparing for the moment it collides hard with the ground. It's a great way for your opponent to score three points and for you to wind up feeling utterly humiliated, not to mention seriously hurt.

That's how I scored my first three points against Totlak. I snapped, turned, thrust, and pulled back, putting a tremendous bind on his neck. It was a beautiful throw, one of those rare ones where timing, strength, and speed all came together perfectly. At once, I circled behind him and he braced himself. I wrapped my arms around his rib cage and began to work for another turn. I faked to one side and then burst to the other. He fell for it and I was able to turn him, exposing his back for another two points. The official blew the whistle and brought us both back up on our feet for the restart.

If there ever was a day when I felt unbeatable, it was then. Everything worked that night and it was as if I simply could not make a mistake. I dominated the match from start to finish and had never felt so free in a match. By the time the fight was over, I had won emphatically: eight to zero. I became the second wrestler from the US ever to win at the prestigious Poddubny tournament, and in that moment I became the unofficial world champion.

I threw my arms up in the air and acknowledged the crowd of wrestling fans. They were cheering and I glanced over to see Anatoly in tears. Great streams of tears raging down his face toward a smile as wide as the Kremlin. That tough, stoic Soviet demeanor had given way to great joy. He was proud of me, and even though I had known it to be true for some time, it took seeing him overwhelmed with emotion like this to let it really sink in to me. My coach was proud of me. The man who was constantly pushing me beyond what I ever thought was possible was content. I had done enough.

The medal really was solid gold, and there were plenty of people who wanted to touch it as I sat throughout the evening's activities that followed the final. Some people offered me good money for it, but the medal was worth more than the gold; it represented years of suffering, sacrifice, and hard work.

I was invited as an honored guest to the banquet for all of the Russian Wrestling Federation and I'd never seen such a great selection of food on offer. They had spared no expense to bring in the best caviar, steaks, wine, and vodka. Every dish was presented as a work of art. Classical musicians, folk singers, and celebrated actors all performed, but what impressed me most was the company I got to sit with. The room was full of past and present wrestling superstars from all over Russia.

Some of the toughest human beings to walk the planet
were at the table that night, and they let me eat as one
of them.

I sat to the right of Anatoly and we talked with
others about the greats of the past. The longer the evening went on, the louder the stories became, and every
tale seemed to go back to the man after whom the
tournament had been named – Ivan Poddubny. A Soviet
wrestler of Ukrainian Cossack descent, he became the
symbol of wrestling in the first
half of the twentieth century.
For almost forty-five years he
wrestled, performed as a strong-
man and trained with 100 pound
kettle bells – like cannon balls
with handles welded on top
– throwing them around as if
they were made of cloth. Poddubny became known around

Ivan Poddubny

the world as the Russian Hercules and the Champion
of Champions and everything from posters to stamps
to movies bore his name. He was the face of wrestling:
a waxed handlebar mustache sitting above a barrel
chest lined by a pair of twenty-one inch biceps. He was
a grappler, a man who refused to give up the fight and
who gave inspiration to Russians throughout one revo-
lution, two world wars and year after year of struggle.
He was a true Russian hero, full of strength and stamina, like one of the strong men of ancient Greece. For
generations, he was the epitome of what it meant to
finish strong. The tournament that bore his name was
no different – the toughest challenge they believed

their wrestlers could face.

"Now you win Poddubny, you must win Olympic Gold!" So many people said that to me that night. At times it sounded like an order, at times like a prediction. Both ways made me smile and nod and mumble my thanks, remembering the long journey that had brought me to this moment. From the time my brother, Joe, and I were just elementary school age, our parents had supported our dream to be Olympic champions. As a wrestling coach, my dad knew what it would take, and he pushed us hard, giving everything to help us make that dream a reality. The 1996 Olympics were just one year away in Atlanta, Georgia. I would be competing on my home turf. I would be ready. I was going to win.

Chapter one

BORN TO WRESTLE

"Get a good warm-up in, son," said my dad for the fourth time. I was trying my best. I'd already jumped rope for a few minutes, my feet tripping like a newborn colt. Then I'd squeezed out a few push-ups and let my arms go limp as Dad laced up my special kid-size black boxing gloves. I hated it when the gloves went on – I felt like I was carrying bowling balls. I was just five years old, but I knew that I shouldn't complain. I had chosen to come here and fight so no matter how nervous I was feeling, I was going to see it through.

I kept on scanning the locker room to see what the other boxers were doing. None of them had their arms hanging limply down by their sides, struggling under the weight of their gloves. None of them looked nervous, either. Not like me. I was a wreck.

With our mom trailing behind, my little brother Joe walked back into the locker room. Like most four-year-olds he was still a little chubby, and when he walked he had a way of sticking his belly out like an old time gunslinger. Given that he was dressed in the same gym singlet and shorts as me, the effect was even more comical. "Where've you been?" I asked.

"Looking at the ring," he said, his eyes widening with delight as Dad laced up his gloves.

"They've got real lights and everything. It's just like you said it would be, Dad."

"That's right boys. Remember, everyone's here to see you both do your best. You're the stars of the show, you're the ones they're here for."

The truth was Joe and I were the youngest competitors by fifteen years; we were far from the stars of the show. It was a Smoker event, an amateur fight night being held in the gymnasium of our local high school. Dad had put the event on in an effort to raise funds for the school's athletic department, of which he was the coach. In another town, in another time, maybe it wouldn't have been possible to draw in a paying crowd to watch ten different pairs of unqualified, mismatched, amateur boxers take to the ring and more than likely get seriously hurt. But this was Homedale, Idaho in 1972, a town made up of hard workers who farmed the land around.

Ours was a community that valued good, hardworking folk; the tougher the work, the better the man. Sports were seen as a great way to form character and instill discipline in children, and my dad was a charismatic man who many in the town admired and respected. He was the local pastor, the local wrestling coach, and the local teacher. So when he promised them a Smoker event, and that he'd put his own two boys in the ring that night, people wanted to come along and see.

Boxing is not just dangerous and painful, it is extremely physically demanding. Fighters will throw anything between sixty and one hundred and fifty punches per round, and when you're not used to it, even throwing punches can be exhausting. Your legs can begin to feel as though you've got molasses running through your veins while your shoulders scream with sharp pain from holding the weight of your gloves and hands up. You can become too tired to throw punches fast enough to hit your opponent, and pretty soon you become too worn-out to pull your hands back and up in defense after you have led with a jab. If your opponent has the energy for a counterattack and you're too tired to get your guard up, you become nothing more than a punching bag on legs. And that moment when you get hurt is the precise moment that makes these Smoker events so much fun to watch. When people box who aren't ready to box, someone's going to get their head knocked off.

Of course, I was convinced I was going to be the one bringing the awe. Even though Joe and I had been wrestling for a couple of years already, I was psyched as we walked out to the boxing ring, a new burst of energy making my iron gloves feel lighter. It looked to me as though the whole town had turned out, which – given that Homedale had a population of 600 – was probably right. We were first on, which in my mind meant that we were absolutely the main attraction.

I learned many things that night. I learned that adrenaline is a great painkiller and a powerful booster. I learned that I loved the sound a crowd makes, how all those voices fuse into one single sound, like a wild musical instrument. And when you find yourself conducting that sound, when something as simple as a punch that you throw landing square on the jaw of your opponent causes the whole room to resonate with cheers and shouts, it feels great. I learned that when I fight, my attention narrows in ways that it never does at any other time. I learned that nothing will get in my way as I unleash every last ounce of my power in pursuit of victory; not even the sight of my little brother with blood gushing from his nose, his eyes swollen and full of tears. I learned that I was a fighter, that as I unleashed my hundredth blow onto Joe's face and the fight got stopped and my hand was raised, I felt good.

Dad rushed us home to the tiny parsonage before I could sign any autographs, watch any of the other matches or revel in my status as champion of the ring. I just had to sit and replay my memories of the sweet victory while Mom and Dad looked worried and applied ice to Joe's swollen face. There was no shouting, but I knew Mom was unhappy and wanted to know why Dad hadn't stopped it sooner.

I knew why he didn't stop it. He didn't stop it because even though there was blood and pain and it must have been horrible for both him and Mom to look at, we were doing exactly what we had set out to do. This was what we had signed up for. He didn't stop it because I was already a little warrior, and warriors finished their own battles.

Like the two generations of Russell boys before me, I was learning that toughness is what little boys must learn on the way to manhood. Life is tough, we were told, and we needed to learn how to take the hard blows it would throw at us.

It didn't take Joe long to recover from his injuries, and even though I was older, taller, and now – as I reminded him often – the official boxing champion of the house, he didn't back away from me. In fact, as much as that night taught me all those lessons, it delivered Joe an even more valuable one: that the ring was no place for someone who was timid. So, as the months passed and we grew older, Joe started to come at me harder than ever, arguing with me, teasing me and refusing to tolerate anything I threw at him.

Dan (3) and Joe (2) in their first of many wrestling singlets.

You have to know that I have always loved my little brother. I loved him and I admired him and I always thought he was the perfect one – an example for me to follow. But he was also sneaky. If ever he didn't know whether something was right or wrong he would get me to go and try it first. I would take the dare, charge on ahead and face the consequences while Joe watched and learned from my mistakes.

Over and over I fell for Joe's cunning ways. He was a master at playing the middle man and he'd wind me up by telling me what other boys said about me behind my back, then do the same thing with them, divulging my own secrets about them. He enjoyed instigating and of course, I was guilty of being easy prey. Because I was less clever emotionally than Joe, I worked out how to get even in other ways. I'd borrow a few dollars from him and then pay him back in pesos, telling him, "Foreign currency is hard to come by, Joe, so you're getting a really good deal here." He wasn't keen, but I wasn't changing my offer. No way.

As we continued to disagree about the payment plan, we reached the inevitable dead end. "There's only one way we can settle this," I told him one afternoon when the argument flared up again.

"What's that?"

"We're going have to fight." This didn't bring about the look of terror that I half suspected it would. Instead, Joe looked very serious and said, "OK, but we have to ask Dad if we can."

Once we had his permission, we set to it. There was no holding back. We pulled hair, scratched deep grooves into each other's skin with our fingernails. We gave each other friction burns from the rugs and used our feet, legs, and knees to strike with full force knowing it was all legal with Dad's approval. We'd learned a few wrestling moves by then and once we had taken the other down we'd rain down the punches. "Do you give up?" one of us would shout, pausing the violence as we sat, pinning the other to the ground. But neither of us ever did. Instead the fight would continue that way until whoever was on top would pause long enough to allow the other one to wriggle free and take their turn unleashing the full force of their punches into their brother's face.

I'm not exaggerating when I say we went on like this for hours. Neither of us would admit defeat, neither would admit weakness, so we carried on, filling the family room with the sound of bone on flesh. My mom hated what we were doing and had taken herself to another room, but Dad just sat there and watched as our lungs began to burn and fatigue took hold of every limb. At one point I felt my nose break and I was struggling to see as my eyes were starting to swell over. My dad sat there. He was a man of his word who had given his permission for us to fight, yet watching the fight in his own home brought back painful memories for him. Drunken brawls were a familiar part of his childhood and he was determined that this would not become a regular pattern for us. As he watched and waited, he was determined that we would learn from this.

I was pouring out blood from several areas of my face and body and my skin had been rubbed raw on the carpet. My ribs were painfully aching and bruised and Joe looked the same. But neither would give up.

"Say you're sorry, Joe!" I'd scream at him.
"No," he'd spit in reply.
WHACK! My fist would connect with his face.
"Say you're sorry!"
Again the "no," and again the punch.

After several hours, I felt a heavy hand on my back, pulling me away from Joe. Dad had finally had enough and stepped in. Making us stand dizzily in front of him, he spoke. His voice was shaking with the effort it required of him to control his emotions. "I never want either of you to treat the other like that again. Ever. You're brothers and you're not to fight like that. Do you understand me?"

"Yes, sir," we both replied.
"Good. Now go and get the belt."

This was the signal that we were to both receive a spanking. We did what we always did when he told us to get the belt and scrambled as fast as our bruised legs would carry us to the bedroom in the back of the house and the corner of Dad's closet. It was always a race to get the thick black leather belt first, and return to Dad ready and willing to submit to the punishment. If you didn't rush toward the beating, you always got far worse.

"You will not forget this," he said after spanking us. There were tears in his eyes, his face flushed red and the veins in his temple pulsing. "You will never treat your brother like that again, ever. This will never happen again."

He was right. Joe and I never fought like that again. The beating we got from Dad was nothing compared to the abuse we had handed out to each other, and even before our bodies were healed from the battle I knew that something had changed between us. A new bond of love and respect had grown between us. We each knew that the other would never give up, that we would fight to the end if necessary. Yes, I'd beaten Joe at the Smoker, but our battle at home had settled it once and for all. We would never need to challenge each other again. We knew that both of us were born to fight.

As much as I loved my brother and adored my mother, my dad was the dream weaver. I loved and respected him for the way he could bring dreams alive within me. He was a magical man who had the ability to turn anything into an adventure. We were poor, like everyone else in the town, but that didn't stop Dad from casting his spell over us as he struggled to find the money to feed us. As the month drew to a close and the money ran out, his magic would grow stronger. "Tonight," he loudly declared in front of near-empty kitchen cupboards, "we're eating Pygmy stew!"

We were intrigued. Neither of us had ever heard of Pygmy stew before, but judging by Dad's wide-eyed big grin, we were in for a treat. "It's a very special meal," he explained, putting everything he could find into the pot on the stove. There was one leftover hotdog in some tomato soup, a few Chinese noodles floating on top and all kinds of weird stuff that neither Joe nor I could identify down at the bottom. Before we were allowed to begin our meal, Dad took down the encyclopedia from the bookshelf and started to read. "The Pygmies in Africa are known for their strength. Scientists have found that this comes from their diet, which consists of a stew that is both highly nutritious and powerfully filling. One bowlful of Pygmy stew is enough to keep a young Pygmy full for a whole week!"

"Do you hear that, boys? A single bowlful will keep you full for a whole week and make you as strong as any warrior. Who wants some?"

Like baby birds with their beaks straining open in the nest we offered up our bowls, begging for an extra large helping. Of course, once we got it in our mouths we found that it was truly vile and disgusting, but that didn't stop us from believing every single word that came from Dad's mouth.

"Oh, yes," we'd both reply. "This Pygmy stew really is amazing, Dad."

"And so filling too!"

It was the same with Swamp Water (lime Kool-Aid without any sugar) and Magic Juice (bottles of juice that magically refilled of their own accord every night). And while the nutritional value of almost all of Dad's creations was dubious at best, they made us strong in other vital ways: we grew to love and trust him even more.

Dad's imagination didn't stop at food. He was a master storyteller, always looking for a fun way to teach us a lesson or give us advice. Because we had no TV but occasionally got to watch it at friends' houses, Dad played on our fascination. Every week we got a phone call from Mr. French from our favorite TV show *Family Affair*. He'd call up to congratulate Joe or I on whatever we had done well that week and to offer us some advice for the days ahead. And most nights we would have our stories read by none other than *Sesame Street*'s own Mr. Snuffleupagus who was very shy and tired from all that filming, so we had to have the lights down low and not try to jump on him as he peeked through the doors of the closet. But we appreciated his time nevertheless.

Give Dad a Bible story and he would make it come alive in ways that I've never seen surpassed even today. We were mesmerized by him, hanging on his every word. We loved him, we trusted him, and we gladly let him weave our dreams for us. Even to this day, I still count myself fortunate to have had such a father.

All of this that my father brought to our lives – the magical living, the dream weaving, the discipline of sport and the importance of being disciplined – was in some way a response to the world my father had experienced himself. The Russells emigrated from Ireland many generations ago, eventually moving from Nebraska out to Idaho, settling in Homedale. My dad's father was a hardworking man, and in the Irish way he liked a drink. They were the poorest family in the town, and there was no shame in either of those facts. I loved my grandpa, with his beer in one hand and a pack of cigarettes permanently in the other.

Born into a poor farming family, my dad was the oldest son of eight children. Grandpa came back from WWII a broken man, and my dad's mother was often sick herself, relying on lengthy lists of prescriptions to keep her going. Home life was tough and Grandpa insisted that each of his children learn the meaning of hard work. So, by the time he was five Dad had his first job working in the fields. It was only when he became distracted by athletics that his work ethic came into question, for as Grandpa often reminded him, "Farming requires the whole family to take part." If Dad wanted to go play sports, he would have to fit them in around his daily chores.

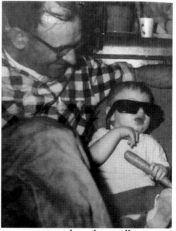

Grandpa Al Russell

Grandpa was a farmer with an iron work ethic, and his only educational requirement was that his children finished the eighth grade. That was all that had been required of him and it was all he expected of his own children. Once they'd passed that milestone, he felt they had all they needed to make their way in the world.

For Dad, athletics provided a distraction from the hard work of farm life, but even though he excelled at sports Grandpa never once chose to leave the bar or the fields to watch his oldest son compete. Not when he captained the football team. Not when he won the state wrestling title. Not when he set state records in track.

Sports – and the coaches who took him under their wing – became a savior for Dad, and when he met Mom it didn't take them long to start dreaming about starting their own family. They knew even then that when they did, they would do things differently. They would never speak a harsh word to their children, they would support everything they chose to do and help them grow up to fulfill every last bit of their potential.

As Homedale changed over the years, my dad stepped into an important role in the community. The place desperately needed hard-working families, as the fields nearby didn't give up their potatoes, barley, and beets easily. Even to this day the largest feature of the town is the migrant camp, which in my childhood housed hundreds of Mexicans – many of them illegal. Families who didn't work hard would starve, and my dad dedicated himself to using sport to give as much support as he could to instilling the proper values in the town's young people.

By the time Joe and I were old enough to take part

in the Smoker event, we were old enough to take on our first jobs. Aged five and four, we were the caretakers for Homedale's only funeral chapel. We mowed the lawns, did all the weeding and kept it well, always under the eye of our father. We were proud of what we did, and so was he. It felt good to know that.

We were out there one day, making sure the lawn edges were perfectly square when I remember my dad sitting us both down. "You know, the greatest gift my father ever gave me was hard work." It made perfect sense at the time, and in so many ways it still does today.

Even though we took part in the Smoker and raged like cage fighters in the living room that day, Joe and I were hooked on wrestling before we could read. We'd go watch Dad coach the high school team and hang on his every word, or sit in the bleachers at tournaments and talk about the best members of the team as if they were warriors from a mythical age. At home, while Dad was at work, we started to practice on each other. Neither of us was getting hurt, so Mom was OK with it, even letting us carry on when she found us using Dad's old jockstraps as head protectors.

"Hey Dad," I called to him one day after he'd gotten back from practice. "Do you want to see me shoot a double leg?" He had no idea how much attention we'd been paying to his words in the gym, and just knowing that his three-year-old boy knew enough about wrestling to be able to correctly name one of the basic moves made him smile.

"Sure, Dan. Show me a double leg."

Joe and I readied ourselves for the demonstration, facing each other on the old rug in front of the couch. I lowered my level, stepped my right foot between Joe's feet and blasted up and threw him, driving him backward onto his back. My dad just stood there, looking shocked. "My turn, it's my turn," said Joe, jumping up from the floor. "Watch me!" We resumed positions, and this time Joe – barely up to my chin – took me down with perfect technique.

Dan and Joe practice wrestling in the living room.

From that day on, we were at every wrestling practice, marching in wearing our matching sweat suits, black singlets, and head protectors – the real deal this time though, not improvised. Dad would beam at us, calling out to the others in the room, "Here come my boys!" It felt good to get so much of his affirmation, so much of his attention. And he was a great teacher.

By the time Joe was five and I was six we knew more wrestling technique than the guys on Dad's high school team.

We grew up as wrestlers. At the dinner table we'd talk about the best way to take someone down, the perfect routines for out-of-season training, and the difference between the two types of Olympic wrestling, Greco-Roman and Freestyle, and which one each of us would take on once we finished the collegiate season.

It was in my sixth winter that Dad took Joe and me along to our first state tournament. The hall was big, far bigger than the school gym in which the Smoker had been held, but my mind immediately went back to that first ever fight of mine. The same adrenaline surge overtook my emotions, the same sense of excitement and expectation as I looked up at the banks of seats and listened to the hum and thrill of the crowd.

There was an under eight division – the youngest category of all – and we were waiting around after we had both weighed in. But while I was straining to get out and fight, Joe was not so sure. Looking upset and hanging back, he finally spoke up, telling Mom and Dad, "I don't want to wrestle."

"Are you sure, Joe?"

He nodded.

"Well, that's OK. You don't have to do this." Looking relieved, Joe went and hid under the bleachers, not putting his head out again until he heard my name called. By then, I was desperate to fight. I shook my opponent's hand and wrestled with even more intensity than usual. Victory came easy, and I stood with my skinny arm held high and a state-sized grin spread across my face. Dad was laughing and clapping with delight and pride in my corner, and I could see Joe standing by Mom at the side of the bleachers, both laughing and celebrating too.

Seeing me win that first match was enough to make Joe want to fight his own, and he quickly got Dad to make sure it was OK for him to still compete. I went on to win all my other matches and walk out of the hall as state champion for my weight division, and so did Joe. We were both state champs together, and it felt out of this world.

For Dad, wrestling was the perfect metaphor for life. He often talked about what it took to be a champion, how important it was to trust the coach and do exactly what he said. And just as we needed a coach for sports, he was also clear that we needed a coach for the rest of life too.

I was sitting next to Dad at church one day not long after becoming state champion when something changed. It was near the end of the service and the preacher was making his passionate call for people to come down to the front and become Christians. Dad was sitting there looking peaceful, but inside I felt my heart pound with all the force that I'd experienced at state. I knew I had to do something, and tugged on his jacket. "Dad!" I whispered. "I want Jesus to be my coach too." His eyes warmed and widened, filling with pride and joy.

"Really? You want that?"

"Yes, I do Dad. I really do."

And so we stood, hand in hand, and walked down to the front, where we knelt and prayed and I asked Jesus to be my coach for life. I wanted it so badly, and I believed with all my heart that this one simple prayer would have an almost magical impact upon my life. I don't know where I got the idea, but I was convinced that from then on my life would be nothing but wonderful and easy.

I couldn't have been more wrong. The magic of my early years seemed to dissipate in the months that followed. Life became complicated, painful, and often traumatic. I found myself struggling with feelings of shame and disgust, trying to cover up these awkward, uncomfortable emotions with bad behavior and daily acts of rebellion.

If it feels as though this came out of nowhere, it's because it really did take me by surprise. All it took was one neighborhood bully to decide to torment me in ways a young boy should not be treated and the damage began. I began acting out to cover up the shame and pain from what was going on, misbehaving at home and encountering frequent spankings as a result. And when my parents started fostering children,

I found that I didn't have the emotional tools to defend myself against their brokenness. Life slipped so quickly from fairy tale to nightmare and I discovered that my life was no longer about wrestling for sport or pleasure in the gym; now I felt as though I had to scrap for my own survival.

It was when Uncle Jeff moved in with us that things started to really go wrong. I knew he was my dad's youngest brother, but I had no idea why he had moved out of Grandpa's home, and I had no idea why he took such an instant and extreme dislike to me. But after just a few weeks I knew that while his beatings were occasional, it was with his words that he made the deepest cuts.

"You're no good, Dan," he'd tell me. "You know why you're always getting into trouble with your dad? It's because you're useless. You're never going to be anything other than useless and your family would be better off without you."

It's hard to shrug off words like these when they come from a teenager who you look up to, who can teach you great wrestling moves, who listens to Led Zeppelin, who talks about taking drugs and who says rude things at dinner that make your mom blush. It's hard to resist the temptation to believe these lies when you've already begun to think them for yourself, when you've already started to know the toxic pain of shame. It's hard to ignore when, deep down in the core of your being, you believe it to be true.

My mind began to play a tape made up exclusively of negative thoughts. I am no good. No one will ever love me. I will grow up and never amount to anything. I built a wall of protection around myself, hoping it would shield me. All it did was encourage my tormentors even more. And the more they taunted me, the more I believed them. The dark voices in my head had engaged the fight and they were winning. The ring grew bigger and I began to shrink from the fight. I tried to disappear and withdraw, but I was failing.

And yet, there was wrestling. There in the gym I could finally breathe. There with the sweat and the pain and the relentless drills to perfect an already great technique, I found some kind of freedom. I longed to hear the approval of the crowd and was desperate for the times when I could soak in the pride of my family after a fight well fought. Wrestling became my obsession, the only way to hush the voices that told me I was worthless.

The more I fought, the more I won. But even though I was a champion with titles and trophies and a growing reputation even at the age of eight, as soon as the sweat dried, the bleachers emptied or the venue disappeared from view, I was back in my world of horror, back with the voices that hated and taunted me.

"No one will ever love you! You will never amount to anything!"

Uncle Jeff was creative in his torture. He dangled me head first from the top of stadium bleachers; he would spit on my face and tie me up in sleeping bags, always coming up with new ways to take out his frustrations on me. And when he decided it was time Joe and I learned to swim, he took us both to a canal and threw us in while he stood on the side and laughed. It turned out that Joe was fine, a real natural swimmer. I, on the other hand, floundered, thrashed and drank half the canal before I finally made it back to the side.

I became a child defined by the great contrast within me. In one area of my life I felt complete, special and loved, but in all other venues I felt afraid and lonely. It was like I had a chasm within me, and only the tiniest shaft of light was visible. I was a swamp with just a small patch of solid ground. I was dead with only the faintest whisper of breath.

Chapter two

THE CARDBOARD BOX

It wasn't just hot the day that my dad struggled through the door with the oversized cardboard box; it was withering. Fourth of July had come and gone, and the combination of a fierce sun and hot winds blowing up from Mexico was searing our little Idaho town. It was too hot to wrestle, but not too hot for Joe and me to jump up and do what Dad said the minute we saw him enter.

"Clear the table, boys," Dad said as he headed for the dining room, struggling with the box that was at least half the size of a washer. He wasn't a tall man, but we never doubted his strength, and judging by the sweat, the heaving breaths and the clipped sentences, whatever was in the box was heavy. Really heavy. Joe and I exchanged glances. We had absolutely no idea what he was up to. How exciting was this?

Once the box was on the table, there was no way on earth Dad was going to pass up the opportunity to entertain and educate us. He waited quietly while Joe and I scrambled around on the floor like puppies at feeding time. "What's in the box, Dad? Lemme see!"

Slowly he began to peel back the lid of the box, his eyes fixed on ours. "Boys, what have I told you about televisions in the past?"

"That we would never have one in our house?" I said.

"Ever," said Joe, his face crumpling in frustration at the memory of all those conversations.

"I know," he said, reaching in. "But something's changed." I was nine years old and I'd never known him to go back on his word, and I found myself caught between two extreme emotions: the sheer joy of hoping that what Dad was about to pull out of the box was an actual television, and the total confusion at hearing him admit that he had changed his mind.

"What's changed?" I asked.

"Yeah, Dad, what's the TV for?" said Joe.

Pulling the great lump of glass, wood and plastic out of the box with all the care of a museum curator, Dad set it down on the table. It was magnificent. Even without it plugged in we were captivated by it: the curve of the glass, the dark reflections that seemed to hide within it, the shine of the wood. It was the most beautiful thing I had ever seen.

"Boys," said Dad, crouching down so our eyes were level with his, dropping his voice to an almost whisper so we had to lean in to catch his every word. "This summer something special's happening. This summer is the Olympic Games!"

To a third grader like me, there was no awareness of the significance of these games. I had no idea that the previous Games in Munich in 1972 had seen eleven Israeli athletes killed by Palestinian terrorists, and I had no clue that the world needed 1976 to restore faith in the Olympics. As for the underlying tensions fueling the Cold War that were being played out as East competed against West, I was oblivious. But I knew anything that got my dad to change his mind and buy a brand new TV had to be important. So I was all in, right from the start, hanging on his every word.

I missed the fact that the Games were marred by boycotts and drug allegations, and that a rainstorm managed to extinguish the Olympic Flame a few days after the opening ceremony. None of that would have mattered anyway, for a stronger flame had been ignited in both my and Joe's heart, the sort that could never be doused.

1976 was the year Romanian gymnast Nadia Comaneci earned her flawless 10 – the first time judges had scored any gymnastic performance as perfect. Then she did it again. And again. Seven times in total she scored a perfect 10, winning three gold medals in total. It was the year Bruce Jenner took gold in the decathlon and the USA boxing team cleaned up with golds going to Leon Spinks, Michael Spinks, Leo Randolph, Howard Davis Jr., and Sugar Ray Leonard.

Yet nothing inspired us quite as much as the wrestling. We didn't miss a second of the action as Dad had borrowed a Betamax video machine from school and taped every wrestling match that ABC showed. For him it was a great tool for gathering teaching material that he would use with his students in the forthcoming season, but for us the lessons were being taught right there and then. For Joe and me, the wrestling matches that were broadcast from those Olympic Games were nothing short of life changing. After the summer of '76, nothing would ever be quite the same.

There were thousands of fans wedged into the wrestling venue for the Games, and as the coverage started, Dad would talk us through the people whose faces appeared on our screen. Exotic sounding names fell from his tongue as he spoke with accents I'd never heard him use before. Men with the thickest facial hair I'd ever seen that grew like desert weeds, deep set eyes that seemed to me to be capable of nothing but menace, shoulders covered in hair like fur. There were men from countries I had heard of – strange, different places like the Soviet Union and East Germany – but there were other country names that must surely have been made up just for fun. Everything about the Olympics captured my attention and fed my imagination.

"Now pay attention," Dad said one day early on, leaning in toward the set and narrowing his eyes. "This guy's something special."

We watched as a man wearing an American singlet took to the mat. We knew enough to be able to tell that he was good and had built up a comfortable lead, but it was what happened between the second and final round that really captured our imagination. Another wrestler, wearing a Team USA sweat suit, approached him and started talking, the camera picking up every word: "You've got to circle more instead of coming straight at him all the time," he said. "This guy is dangerous." The first wrestler nodded, went back out and carried on, circling his opponent as he had been told.

Once the match was over and the American had won, we turned to Dad for an explanation. "Those two wrestlers are brothers; the Peterson brothers. They're always looking out for each other and they're just like you two: brothers who love to wrestle."

As if that wasn't enough to get us hooked, the stories Dad started to tell about them made Joe and me instant fans of the Petersons. "Just like you there's only one year between John and Ben, and just like you lots of people used to think they were twins."

Dad was right about that. People were always asking whether Joe and I were twins, especially as I had been held back so I could start school at the same time as my little brother, allowing us to go through the difficult transition together. We had soon grown tired of people asking whether we were twins and found that if we answered with, "We're not twins, we're triplets, only our third brother died," people generally stopped asking.

"They grew up like you, in farming country,"

explained Dad. "Only they're from Wisconsin and their parents owned a dairy farm out in Comstock. They grew up working hard, milking cows, stacking bales of hay and working at a local cannery. I tell you, these are two of the toughest wrestlers ever to walk on our planet."

I had no reason to doubt him. We listened as Dad told us how they had caught the wrestling world's attention four years earlier in Munich with Ben winning gold and John getting silver. In Montreal, the brothers scrapped for every victory and wound up with John winning gold and Ben silver.

I loved seeing John, having just won his final match, run over to stand at the side of the mat and watch and cheer as his little brother fought. "When you've got a brother in it with you," John said afterward, "it's hard getting all wrapped up in yourself."

I remember Ben talking about his earlier win in Munich, how he thought, "This medal is going to change my life." "It did," he said, "but I found out that kind of success wasn't enough. The only thing that brings true happiness is following God's plan."

Television. Wrestling. Olympics. God. Two warrior brothers united in their support of each other. Sitting with my brother and my dad as we watched the matches unfold and talked about the great things we were seeing. It was a summer I'll never forget. It was a summer that confirmed the path Joe and I were convinced we were going to follow: in the footsteps of John and Ben Peterson, we were going to wrestle our way to the Olympics.

Summer passed and the fall began to take hold, but Joe and I remained focused and determined. We were still holding our Olympic finals in the family room, still arguing over who had won gold and who had won silver. We were still running victory laps with arms held high, still plotting ways of getting an even better takedown.

For us, wrestling was fuel for our imagination, but for my dad wrestling was a tool to raise men. He was not trying to make us into world beaters or tiny clones of himself and he had no desire to be another of those fathers screaming from the sidelines. He just wanted us to learn how to grow up to be men. That was his calling as a father. It was his passion.

But he was also realistic about what it took to succeed in the ring. One night, as Dad watched our Olympic play, he called us over. "I love watching you play like this, but I wonder whether you realize just how significant it was that John and Ben Peterson won those medals. What they did took blood, sweat, tears, time, effort, work, discipline, dedication, self-control... Without a full commitment to each and every one of those, they'd never have made it. Do you understand what I'm saying?"

I nodded my head, but I really didn't have a clue. How could a nine-year-old appreciate the sacrifices that would have to be made over so many years in

order to even get to the Olympics, let alone win? To
Joe and me it was all a dream, but that didn't mean we
didn't believe it was possible. To us it was the most
exciting adventure we could ever hope to set out on. Of
course we had no idea what it would cost, no idea how
we would have to change if we were to complete the
journey. But perhaps we did learn one thing that night:
when we wrestled, it made Dad happy.

Two weeks later, as yet another Olympic final was
played out on the thick carpet of the family room – this
time with Joe taking gold thanks to a quick double leg
that had caught me off guard – Dad spoke up again.
"I've been thinking, and I wanted to ask you both
something."

He looked more serious than usual. There was no
dance in his eyes like when Mr. Snuffleupagus was
about to come out or the Pygmy stew was being served
up. Not that he looked sad either, just serious. We knew
that whatever he had to say was important. We sat
down in front of him, still trying to catch our breath
from the fight.

"Do you want to be the best wrestlers in the world?" I
didn't have to look at Joe to help me work out what my
response should be, though when I glanced at him, I
saw he was nodding just as much as I was. "Yes, Dad," I
said. And with that, our Olympic pursuit began.

We had a long way to go, and Dad had his work cut
out for him as our coach. He'd been a great sports-
man in his own youth and had been working with high

school students as soon as he finished his college years. He had taken that same magic that had inspired us at so many mealtimes and bedtimes and made the sport come alive for the young men.

He was able to get the best out of his athletes. Before an important meet with a rival high school he brought in a tray of cream puffs and read aloud a note he pretended was from their opponents. "They sent you these because they think you're a bunch of cream puffs," he told them. "Are you going to stand for that?" It was kind of silly, but it did the job.

When students made mistakes – whether in the ring or out of it – he would tell them how to put it right. He never passed up an opportunity to shape a young man's character, and winning medals and trophies was never his ultimate aim. For Dad, the goal was instilling in his boys a love of hard work, discipline, dedication, and self-control that would last way beyond their wrestling days.

So he'd never experienced anything like the kind of planning and expertise required to get an athlete to be able to compete on the global stage. Dad being Dad, he went about it with all the usual passion, fun, and creativity that he could.

We had morning calisthenics and he set us daily goals, like completing the three-mile running course he had mapped out for us and doing one hundred sit-ups and one hundred push-ups. He'd time us as we ran and check that we had completed our tasks, and we never dreamed of not completing them. We were wrestlers, and wrestlers never lied or snuck out of training.

Dad managed to weave John and Ben Peterson's story into our own. He painted a picture of what they did to become great, reminding us that this pain and discomfort and hard work we were experiencing was the exact same pain, discomfort, and hard work they had pushed through, day after day after day.

"Is that really what you want?" he would ask.

"Yes," we'd shout. "YES!"

"Then you're going to follow through on this commitment."

Our belief in our dream – and our dad's ability to get us there – was unshakable. But if you had seen us then you would not have considered even for one moment that we were in any way serious about our Olympic aspirations. I was the skinniest guy in my class and my thick glasses refused to stay on my nose. I wore hand-me-downs from church parishioners and looked like one of those archetypal wimps that are just waiting to get sand kicked in their face. The biggest part of my arms was my elbows, while the biggest part of my legs was my kneecaps. Joe was just the opposite. He was the shortest and heftiest guy in our class. Fatso and Skinny Bones, that's what they called us.

Yet we believed. Every recess, as Fatso and Skinny Bones we took ourselves outside and found a place to carry on doing our sit-ups and push-ups. We attracted strange looks, muffled laughs and out and out ridicule. Fatso and Skinny Bones were headed to the Olympics, wasn't it funny? But we believed and there was no way to change our minds.

Dan, Grade 2

In fact, the worse the ridicule, the fiercer the belief. I became obsessed with wrestling, and it became the filter through which I viewed everything else. Any problems in my life were like opponents that had got me in a hold; all I had to do was work out how to get out. And opposition or ridicule were just more pains I had to work my way through, not walk away from.

When I was six years old we moved a few miles north from Homedale to Wilder, Idaho, a town with an even smaller population. It's still a farm town today, the sort where you're just as likely to see a tractor or a farm truck on the road as a car. And just like Homedale most of the population was Hispanic immigrants who were there to work the fields. Joe and I were gringos, and it wasn't a term of endearment.

Most days I would hear the same greeting floating out toward me across the school corridors: "Hey Gringo, Loco–moco en la cabeza!"

"No!" I'd call back, wearily. "I am not a gringo with

crazy boogers in my head." But it never seemed to help.

Fair skinned, skinny and looking like a librarian's orphan, I was painfully aware that I was an outsider. I was different. I was as good as worthless. The dark voices in my head got louder.

I felt as though I was always on the outside. The one time the racial barriers came down was when there was a game of marbles going on. It didn't matter what color your skin, what mother your tongue or what style your clothes; when it came to marbles it was every man for himself. It was serious business. We played for keeps out there on the playground, and if your marble was tagged it would no longer be yours. I lost a lot of marbles throughout the years at Holmes Elementary in Wilder, Idaho, and once I joined the third grade the games grew even more hostile, with bad losers nearly always hitting out. I learned to take a punch in those early years.

It wasn't just the marbles that caused the fists to fly. When it came to Noel Rodriguez, all it took was for me to open my mouth.

Noel was a year ahead of me at school, and he was the toughest guy in the whole place. Having a younger kid mouth off about wanting to be an Olympic champion was obviously too good to resist, and he found me one day early on in the year, shouting my name from across the playground. "Hey Skinny Bones! You think you're gonna win some kind of medal at the Olympics, do you?"

"Yes," I said, cursing the talent I had been born with for finding abuse.

"How about we give you a little practice, huh?" Marching over toward me, blowing his cheeks and narrowing his eyes, he walked straight up and slugged me hard in the stomach. Another blow followed soon after that, leaving me winded and half-slouched on the ground.

And so began our new daily routine. Noel would call out my name, tease me about my Olympic aspirations, and lay just enough punches on me to send me down, leave me gasping for breath or cause enough commotion for a teacher to come over and investigate. Thanks to the epic battle with Joe I knew fighting with my fists was not the answer, but I had also listened hard in Sunday school, especially when Jesus told people to "turn the other cheek." I figured Jesus was my coach in life, so I had better do what he said.

It lasted throughout the semester, but perhaps it wasn't all bad. After all, I was learning how to take a punch and how to avoid getting distracted by the cheers and shouts of a hostile crowd. I learned how to fall and how, if I went down too early, Noel's punches would be followed with a few swift kicks. But as much as my body was getting toughened up, my soul was being weakened with every fight. Each strike, each laugh and jeer from the crowd reinforced the message that I was no good, unlovable, pathetic.

I was dreaming of being a champion in the ring, but

recess taught me I was a loser in life. These thoughts hurt far more than the kicks and punches. And because Noel never seemed to tire of the fighting, my inner rage began to build. Months passed and I had yet to return a punch, but gradually I built up enough anger within me to force me to act. So I spoke to my dad. I told him all about Noel, how the beatings had been going on since the start of the year. "And I've never hit him back, Dad. Never. I've turned the other cheek every time. But now I want to fight him. Will you let me?"

Dad had given me permission to fight just once before, and I felt nervous asking him for a second time. But he surprised me with his reaction. "Yes," he said. "You can fight, but fight with honor."

I went to bed that night full of the kind of relief and excitement that typically comes on Christmas Eve. But this was better than Christmas. This was about revenge and honor and changing everything I hated about my life. I struggled to get to sleep, but when I did I saw myself standing in the middle of the schoolyard, face to face with Noel. I watched the epic encounter play out again and again, perfecting the speech I would give in front of the whole school:

"Noel," I'd say, standing eyeball to eyeball with my tormentor. "I want to be your friend," (I'd feel particularly Christ-like at this point) "but if you touch me again, you will be picking yourself up in a thousand different pieces!"

A familiar look of anger and disdain would fall across

his face and he'd get ready to strike. But I would be too quick. I'd beat the living tar out of him, my speed, reach, and accuracy leaving him bloodied and wounded on the floor while the whole school gathered and cheered. I pictured myself being carried away in victory, high on the shoulders of the oldest boys in the school, never to be challenged on the playground again. I listened as I gave a speech about how I'd tried turning the other cheek but Noel had left me no choice but to end it this way.

The scene was on constant repeat in my dreams that night, and I woke the next morning with the script word-perfect in my mind. I attacked the morning calisthenics with extra vigor, ate breakfast twice as fast and hurried to school eager to get into battle. This was going to be the day I would show him I was made of championship material. This was going to be the day my Olympic dream would draw a whole lot nearer.

I couldn't concentrate on my studies and was counting the minutes until the recess bell sounded. My heart rate rose every time I rehearsed the fight and the speech in my mind, and there was no doubt in my mind that I would emerge victorious. I knew I had taken his best punches for the better part of a year and there was no way at all that he could hurt me more than he already had. And while I knew everything about Noel's power, he knew nothing at all about mine. He was about to encounter the power punch of a skinny but determined third-grader.

The bell rang. I marched off to our usual fighting

place on the playground – a corner where the adult supervisors had never once disturbed us – and went through a few gentle warm-ups to try and channel the adrenaline. I could feel my focus narrowing. I was ready. And when Noel arrived I walked straight up to him, got our eyeballs as close as I'd seen them in the dream and, with great confidence, delivered my first line. "Noel, I want to be your friend, but if…"

"OK," he said, his hand reaching out to shake mine. Then he turned away and left me. No speech, no fight, no crowd, no revenge. I had never been so disappointed. I wanted to fight. I wanted to prove myself to the whole school, to show that I could stand up for myself and end these beatings by using my own strength. Instead, it felt as though Noel had just gotten bored or had enough.

Noel was true to his word and the beatings never happened again. But my pride was wounded and my soul conflicted. I'd done what I thought was the right thing for so long; I'd chosen to let the bully have his way and not sink to his level, and where had it gotten me? I didn't even have the chance to fight and show what I could do. What kind of champion lived like that?

Chapter three

FLIP THE SWITCH

Of the three movies that played a significant role in my childhood, there is one that I have absolutely no memory of. I was just one year old the day Mom, Dad, and I took a trip to the drive-in movie theatre, too young to be able to remember what I saw through the windshield as I sat on the back seat of our orange VW bug with black racing stripes. But I know that at some point during Planet of the Apes, Mom's water broke and she went into labor. A few hours later I was greeting Joe for the first time ever.

I must have been five or six when we all took a trip back to the same outdoor theatre to see my second movie: Lady and the Tramp. Again the memories are not as sharp as I would like them to be, but of this one I do remember the dread fear that settled within my stomach as the two Siamese cats filled the screen. To me they were the most fearful thing I had ever seen, the purest depiction of evil possible. Their masks of innocence only made their cruelty more apparent, and for weeks they became the figures that stole into my dreams and raged through my sleep. Only, they were not just the cats from some Disney movie; my subconscious fused them with Noel, Uncle Jeff, and many of my other tormentors.

But while the first gave me a brother and the second gave me fear, it was the third movie I ever saw that played the most significant role in my life.

"Come on," Dad said one afternoon. "We're going for a drive." There was no need to ask where or why – going out on a genuine adventure was a rare occurrence that neither Joe nor I would ever want to spoil. So we sat in the back as Dad pointed the VW bug south and then east, away from Wilder and out across the flat plains that threatened never to end.

The excitement all got to be too much for us after a few miles, and we started begging him and Mom to tell us what it was all about. "You'll see," was the only answer we got until an hour had passed and we entered Nampa, Idaho, eventually pulling up outside a large mall that looked bigger than the whole of Wilder itself. We raced off from the car, sprinting to see who would be first into the mall.

Dad called us back and to attention. He didn't want our youthful passion to let us miss out on the significance of the moment. "Boys, we're going to the movies, and what you're about to see is going to be important for your training. Movies are fun, but this one is extra special."

And it was. It was more than just entertainment. We sat through Rocky like students at the feet of Einstein.

We caught every line and shared every punch. We abandoned ourselves completely to the story of the Italian Stallion. It was a classic tale of the American Dream, a poor young man who starts out as an average, hard-working guy just trying to get by who gets the opportunity of a lifetime to compete on a world stage.

Joe and I loved every minute of it. Never mind that this was boxing and we were wrestlers; what we saw on the screen had so many echoes of our own lives and hopes. The training; the grizzled coach; the ridicule from people who couldn't believe that he could dare to dream; the impossible odds lined up against him and the refusal to give up or back down. And at the close of the fight that brings the film to its climax, with the battle described as "the greatest exhibition of guts and stamina in the history of the ring," Joe and I were on our feet just like the crowd on the screen.

The drive home was every bit as magical as the film. We talked about how we were both going to drink raw eggs every day from now on. We talked about how great it was to see that not having any money was no barrier to success. We talked about winning and training and fighting and never giving up even though our bodies might get broken and beat up and the pain might be almost unbearable. We would not give up on this dream. Ever.

Pulling in back home Dad paused before getting out of the car. It was no small matter that we had all just been to the movies and used two hour's worth of fuel to do it. Money was tight and this kind of extravagance only served to underline the importance of the evening. "Look at me, boys," he said. "If you want to do on the wrestling mat what Rocky did in the ring, you've got to remember that this is what it takes – nothing less than all you have."

The combination of what we had seen on our TV and that one night in Nampa made a significant impact on both Joe and me that year. Like fingerprints at a crime scene, the footage of the Peterson brothers fighting united in Montreal and the lonely figure of the mumbling boxer running the streets of Philadelphia left both of us deeply moved and profoundly inspired. We were going to wrestle, as brothers, giving it all we could, until the very end. That was our dream. That was our pact.

For me, though, it wasn't just Rocky's training sequences and 15 round fights that I liked. He may have shown potential in the ring, but outside he was awkward, misunderstood, and shy. He was the underdog, just like me.

We were all underdogs though. Even my parents. They had married young, having fallen in love during their senior year in high school. Dad came from a poor family and Mom lost her own dad while she was in high school. Neither of them was going to let their circumstances define them. Both of them wanted to rise above their challenges. So when Dad was named captain of the football team and Mom, the cheerleader, was christened Homecoming Queen, it was as if the planets were aligning to bring them together. Within a year they were married and within two years they had me.

Motherhood dominated my mom's early adult years. Not only was she a mother to Joe and me, but to 32 foster brothers and sisters during the first 11 years of my life. Dad was busy teaching, coaching and even pastoring a local church while Mom cared for the home and all the young lives streaming in and out the doors. Home was more of a community center than a traditional family home, with constant activity taking up every inch of the house 24 hours a day. Dad and Mom believed in generosity, and wanted to make a home for kids that didn't have a fair shot at life.

So many of the kids that lived with us had been severely damaged in life. They required large amounts of love and time and because there would be anywhere from two to six of them living with us at any one moment, finding enough time for all of us was difficult for Mom.

Joe and I continued to make our goals throughout our first ten or eleven years, and as we gave ourselves over more fully to the structure and discipline of training – and Mom and Dad continued to have high expectations of our behavior – it only seemed to remind some of our foster brothers and sisters of how different this new family was to their own. It would take a great deal of patience and Mom would work to help each child through this period of adjustment. It didn't always work.

Some of the foster brothers and sisters would be

incredibly charming at first, but as the shock of the transition wore off, many started acting out, often keeping up their good appearance in front of our parents, but unleashing their pain on Joe and me. Night times were the worst.

At times the bedroom that Joe and I shared would be stuffed wall to wall with mattresses with as many as six of us kids sleeping in the small room. Joe and I would listen to chilling stories about sex and violence that would often last into the late night hours. Both of us would struggle to fall asleep on nights like those, the fear too strong for us to relax.

It was complicated and it was messy, though to my young mind it was just normal. I was aware that this was a family duty, a task which we could carry out in an effort to rescue these kids who had been left so troubled and scarred by a broken world. But while I agreed that this was a good thing to do, I couldn't contain my fear, my anger, or my sadness. I became awkward at home, clingy to my mom and whining and crying whenever I felt attacked. And because Dad would not put up with whining or crying, the beatings increased, fueling my belief that all this mess was in some way my own fault.

While our foster brothers and sisters shared our food, TV, bedroom, and yard, they didn't get to share our love for wrestling. That always seemed to be reserved just for Joe and me. Out on the mat or on the way to or from training or a tournament were the only times when we could be sure of having our parents' full attention. And because it felt to me as though wrestling was the sole area of success in my life, I devoted myself to it even more fully.

I'd first competed at the state championships when I was 6, and I hadn't lost the title since then. In my mind that made me a champion already, but Mom and Dad both knew that if Joe and I were going to improve, we'd have to fight tougher battles than we were getting in Idaho.

At the end of the fourth grade, the solution started to present itself. After practice one day Dad sat Joe, Mom, and me down and laid it all out on the line. "I've been offered two new jobs. One's in Portland to pastor a church, and the other's a long, long way away in an Arab country called Yemen. They want me to teach the children of American diplomats. We need to make a decision together."

None of us said a whole lot at this point. I was thinking that Yeah-man sounded like it might be OK, but I didn't like the idea of getting bullied by the kind of kids whose parents made laws and had security guards and such.

Dad outlined the benefits, explaining how he would be working with the children of diplomats, how we would all get the chance to live in a foreign culture and how the whole thing was a great opportunity. Portland would give us the chance to experience life in a metropolitan city, a city which also happened to be home to the best wrestling club for grapplers our age in the nation.

None of us could decide, and as the days slipped by the topic started to get a little more urgent. Dad sat us down again. "We have to come to a decision. But I also believe that God will direct our path. So let's pray..."

After we had all said Amen, Dad pulled out a coin from his pocket and said, "If it lands on heads we will move to Yemen and if it is tails, we will move to Portland."

And that was it. A quick prayer and a flip of a coin were going to determine everything about where we lived. It seemed as good as any idea to me. I watched the coin spiral up and back down toward Dad's hand. Those hands had always looked so big to me, and I didn't find it hard to trust them to catch the coin the right way up. Mom, Joe, and I crowded in on Dad, eager to see what decision had been made for us. With a quick "Here goes," Dad pulled away his covering hand and revealed the coin. "Tails!" we all yelled at once. We were moving to Portland!

Everything was going to change. Mom and Dad promised that for the next years they would focus solely on us. There would be no more foster brothers and sisters, just the two of them and the two of us and a whole lot of wrestling. We moved into a home in the suburbs of Portland, the biggest tri-level home I had ever lived in. Those 2200 square feet felt like a mansion, and compared to the four-roomed church parsonages we had lived in before I guess it was.

But there was more to the home than the size, the

fact that we finally had our own bedrooms or the fact that Dad converted the family room into a wrestling room, painting one whole wall with the Olympic rings and the words "The Olympic Challenge". What really made the difference was the fact that Mom dedicated herself to making home the safe place we always longed for it to be. She reengaged her nurturing, loving inner cheerleader and cared for her two boys full-time. And we needed it, for the challenge that we walked into was our toughest yet.

We arrived at USA Oregon Cobra Wrestling Club in the afternoon. "Remember boys," Dad said for the hundredth time as we pulled up outside, "this is the premier wrestling club in the country. There's no place better for you to learn than here."

The whole club fell under the rule of Coach Sprague, a balding man with an oversized comb over who demanded attention with the passion in his voice and the intensity of his gaze. He watched carefully as a few wrestlers were starting their warm-ups, issuing a few commands here and there. The walls of the gym were covered with the names of national and state, world and Olympic champions who had come up through his program. "Three years with Coach Sprague and you can climb to the top of awards stands," whispered Dad as we walked up to meet him.

I could tell Dad was proud of his boys, not just because he started by listing our achievements as Idaho state champions, but because he was using way more words than he usually did. Coach Sprague just smiled, nodded, and shook our hands. "How about you show me what you've got, boys," he said, inviting us on to the mats. Joe and I did as we had discussed in the car on the way over and ran through a few moves together, all the while with me thinking, "We'll show these big city kids what some small town Idaho boys can bring!"

After we had gone through our full repertoire of moves, Coach Sprague smiled. "How about you boys stay on for today's practice?"

We agreed, our confidence boosted even further. We'd shown him our basics, but just wait until he saw us unleashed on the other kids. No wonder he was smiling.

Turned out that his smile wasn't a smile of joy at having found two potential Olympic athletes. It was in anticipation of the collision that our gold medal egos were about to have with reality.

Never, in all my life, have I been as humbled as I was on that day. There was not one wrestler in the room that my skills could match. We had been used to beating kids two and three years older than us in Idaho, but here in Portland we were getting creamed by kids that much younger. Joe and I both took a beating that afternoon, and as we slouched out of the room and back into the car, it was clear that all three of us could feel the bruises to our egos. No one said a word. What could be said? Our fantasy of becoming wrestling champs was shattered that day. The one thing that I had been holding on to during the early years of abuse at home and at school was now exposed for what it really was: just a little kid's dream.

The next day, after school, Dad loaded us back up into the car. No words again, just a silent car ride back into the city. We were delivered to Coach Sprague, rolled out on the mats yet again for another beating. Again we were the worst wrestlers in the room, only this time, the sense of shock was gone.

This became our daily routine, with Dad taking us after school to take part in the practice that started at 3:30 (which meant getting there at 3:15 and not a moment later) and finished at 7:30. He never asked whether we wanted to do it – perhaps he was scared of what our answer might be. But every day he took us, six days a week, waiting while we failed and failed and failed again.

Others came and went, unable or unwilling to put themselves through the pain and discipline that were required to make it through Coach Sprague's program. "Either get tough or quit," he'd say, often more than a dozen times each practice. He wasn't the only one doing the shouting; we had our own lines to deliver as well. Whenever we entered the room we had to fill our lungs with air and shout, "The making of a champion is an intense burning desire!"

Once across the threshold we knew that the next four hours would test us to our limits. There was no talking, only Coach and his assistants spoke. A raging furnace hung in the corner, forcing stifling hot air into the room, helping to increase the intensity of the conditions, making us sweat constantly, forcing us to dig even deeper throughout.

I was uncoordinated, my muscles unable to keep up with my ever-lengthening bones. Everyone in the room was stronger, meaner, and tougher than me and the techniques being taught just seemed much too strenuous for my thin, frail body.

This was another level of wrestling compared to that which I'd experienced back in Idaho. But even though I was struggling inside the USA Oregon Wrestling room, I started to see some success outside the practice room. I started to medal in the local tournaments, but my feet rarely made it to the top of the award stand. This was good, right? This was progress?

Wrong. In our club it was unacceptable. We were a team of champions and anything less than first place was a failure. A second place finish in a tournament would be reprimanded and your week of training would be hell. So often I found myself placed in the middle of the mat for several hours while Coach would have a fresh wrestler rotate in on me. Every minute, a highly skilled, vigorous opponent would attack me with vengeance. If they did not attack aggressively enough, then Coach would have them join me in the middle and share the same punishment.

"Get tough or go home!" he'd shout. "Get tough or go home!"

I never spoke of quitting, but for what felt like forever I thought about it every day. I was unable to even
score a takedown in the room and so many days I cried
all the way to practice, knowing that I was going to get
beat on, and cry all the way home knowing that the
same thing was awaiting me the next day. It was just
like third grade with Noel, where I was powerless to
defend myself. Only this time, I wasn't just suffering in
silence; Dad, Joe, and Mom could all see how poorly I
was performing. To almost everyone it must have been
clear that this wasn't the sport for me. And though
Mom listened and gave me hugs and was my cheerleader, she could only ease the bruises. Nothing could
address the deeper wounds – the feeling that I was
letting her, Dad and Joe down; that if I was just better at
all this then happiness would return.

Dan and Joe Russell, Grade 5

I'd look at the wall in the family room at home and stare at the words my dad had so carefully painted. The Olympic Challenge was clearly too much for me. But Dad didn't see it that way. Through all the beatings he saw something greater taking shape. Even though I felt like I was falling apart, his passion and belief in me never wavered. Every practice was a step closer to the goal of being a champion, every defeat in the room was a lesson that I would one day draw on.

Our training stepped up, with Dad introducing a new task to complete on the way back from practice. The first time it happened I was crying as usual, feeling tired after four hours on the mat without a single move to feel proud of. "I got you something," said Dad, as he pulled over a few miles away from home. Out of the trunk he pulled Joe's and my running shoes. "If you want to beat the others in the room, you've got to work harder than the others in the room. Put 'em on, boys. You're running home from here."

As well as a five-mile run every evening, when we got home there would be more to do. Dad would often video our practices and we would sit and watch our technique as every position and attack was scrutinized. After that Joe and I would go to the family room where a wrestling mat now covered the floor from wall to wall. Dad would walk us through the steps, guiding us toward a perfected technique. Over and over we would drill one position or technique until Dad was satisfied. "Get tough or go home!" he'd say, just like Coach. Only going home wasn't an option.

Dan, Joe and their father, Rick Russell at a regional national tournament.

For three years, success seemed to elude me, but even though Coach was honest about my failings and harsh with his reprimands, he too would always have words of inspiration. "Think about the bamboo plant, boys. It might grow an inch annually, but then suddenly it can grow 90 feet in 90 days. Like they say, the first year it sleeps. The second year it creeps. The third year it leaps. The first few years that you're in this room you won't think there's any growth at all. But if you stay here and work hard, it'll come."

We'd be drilling and his voice would shout out the question, "Does bamboo grow 90 feet in 90 days?"

"No!" we'd all reply. "It grows 90 feet in 3 years and 90 days."

Coach could squeeze more wisdom out of a simple plant metaphor than anyone I've ever met. "The bamboo plant doesn't just give up when little growth is visible," he'd say. "But what you cannot see during those early years is the root system that it's developing to support all that rapid growth to come. It's maturing itself underground, reaching deep down to get every single bit of goodness and strength that it can from the soil around it." Sometimes he'd realize that he'd lost us a little and would pull us back with some good old-fashioned shouting. "Prepare the ground!" he'd say. "Our culture today is looking for the quick fix and if it does not happen quick then they quit. The bamboo tree does not give up. Champions do not give up or give in!"

Wrestling was a part of Joe and me, and unlike other kids who were pursuing their parents' dream, we were the ones driving ourselves forward, with both our parents alongside us, in full support. I hadn't lost all my self-belief from the Idaho wrestling days, and I chose to believe Coach's words, just like I believed my dad.

Coach Sprague had brought in other coaches to help develop the program, including Pavel Katsen, a Russian that had yet to learn much English but he knew the language of the sport like nobody else. It was all part of the plan to end the Russian domination of the sport – not that I was aware of any of that. All I knew was that Coach Katsen pushed me as hard as

Coach Pavel Katsen

Coach Sprague and as hard as Dad. He'd learned enough phrases to teach us the fundamentals that drove the

Russian wrestlers: "If you not exhausted when you finish, I get mad... you must find way to win!... Russian wrestlers always on limit. If you break that limit, you break man."

"You must be tiger," he'd shout, calling out of us a vicious killer animal, unleashing our murderous instincts as soon as we got on the mat. He taught us that the mental side is more important than the physical. He told us to reach in and find deep inner rage.

I liked what he said, but most of the time all I found within me was a deep inner fear of failure. My nemesis was Larry Gotcher, a stronger, more intense, more technically gifted bully from Washington State. Whenever we met in local tournaments he beat me, often throwing me around at will. It got so bad that when we met in a regional tournament, my legs were shaking so badly I could hardly stand.

It wasn't all bad, and I was getting medals. I was consistently beating everyone I met in tournaments; just not Larry. However, for Coaches Sprague and Katsen, second wasn't what we were aiming for.

"Dan," Coach Katsen would often say to me, "you are too nice. You cry too much. You must become tiger!" Was I physically strong? No. Did I have a better technique? No. But when I heard him talk about a tiger and inner strength and becoming a vicious killer, I could finally say "yes."

After watching me cry for three years Coach Katsen

sat me down one day. He knew the guts of a champion and he knew the look of a fighter. "Dan, you smart boy. Be doctor. Be lawyer. Wrestling no goot for you."

I was crushed. My dream had held up for so long – to ridicule from recess bullies and endless beatings on the mat and Coach Sprague calling me out for not winning my matches. But not now. This was too much. The one coach who I thought was able to fully understand me, the one coach that knew what champions looked like, was telling me that it was over.

It was exactly what I needed to hear. The Peterson brothers had found their inner animal. Rocky had the eye of the tiger. I had to find to my inner champion, my inner warrior or my dream was over. The words I had shouted six times a week for the past three years rattled in my head, "The making of a champion is an intense burning desire."

I had the desire, but was it intense enough? Was the flame fierce enough? I thought long and hard about my dream; for days I asked myself whether I had it in me to fight like Coach Katsen described. Then it hit me. Sitting on the mat in the family room at home, alone, I found myself listening to new words that entered my head.

I thought, "For three years my teammates have given me their best shots and I have not beaten them. Coaches have encouraged me to get tough or quit. I have been through more beatings than I ever thought possible. And I am still here."

That was the day I decided that losing could not hurt me anymore. I had not quit, and that was proof enough that I wanted to win. People had tried to make me stop, and they had failed because I was still here. I had not quit. I would not quit.

All those years of abuse and bullying had made me tough. All of it had made me resilient. While I'd been looking all along for evidence that I was going to start winning, what I had missed was the fact that I was not scared of losing. And that made me free. That was my tiger.

Change can come quickly in life, and thanks to a mixture of numerous humiliations at the hands of Larry Gotcher, the instruction of my coaches, and my dad's belief in me, I learned to control fear rather than be owned by it. I learned new ways of resisting the urge to let my thoughts run away with themselves and my body fall into panic. I learned to breathe, reminding myself that I loved wrestling; that if I embraced the struggle and embraced the fight then winning would take care of itself. I was beginning to learn that if you worry about winning and fear losing, you're going to hate the sport. There will always be wins and losses, incredible highs and aching lows, but learning to love to wrestle, to engage in the struggle, to take hold of that – that's what makes champions.

Larry Gotcher places 1st at 1979 USWF Nationals. Dan is 2nd.

That was the day the switch flipped within me. I went to practice, shouted, "The making of a champion is an intense burning desire!" with more volume and strength than I had ever managed before, and I scored my first practice room takedown. And then another, and another.

Once I had turned the corner in the practice room, it didn't take long for me to start applying it in competition. And when I finally beat Larry Gotcher early on in the next season, I knew there was no going back. I fought for every hold and every inch of the mat and I could tell the moment when he started to worry that he might be about to lose to a skinny freshman – who he has never lost to before – in front of all these col-

leges. Some wrestlers will start to hit out at you when they're fearful like this, others will tense up, while some just get a terrified look in their eyes. Whatever the sign, that's the time to flip the switch, throw the intensity up and push on. I beat Larry by one point. It was the smallest of margins, but enough to tell me that I had broke through. From then on I knew that I owned him.

I had flipped the switch. There was no way I was turning it off.

Chapter four

THE GLIMPSE FROM THE TOP OF THE WORLD

"Uncle Jeff's coming back to stay with us," Mom announced at breakfast one morning. While the conversation carried on as normal – Joe asking where Uncle Jeff had been, Dad reminding him about Jeff's three year tour in the Army, Mom wondering what kind of thing he'd like to eat for his first meal back at home with us – my mind was elsewhere.

I was thinking about the two years Uncle Jeff had stayed with us back in Idaho. He was fourteen then, I was five and he had made my life a cruel hell. From the two years that he stayed with us there were so many memories to choose from: painful comments whispered so only I could hear them, lengthy discourses on the breadth and depth of my failings, bags of candy that he forced Joe to eat in front of me but was not allowed to share.

But I was no longer a grade school age outsider who was getting bullied at home or at school. It had been three years since we had invited anyone to come and live with us, and thanks to the attention and devotion of Mom and Dad I was a long way from that awkward child so full of insecurity. Besides, I had learned to fight. I had chosen to embrace the struggle and not give up. Why, Coach Sprague himself had even begun to compliment me on some of my technique, calling me out to demonstrate in front of all the others. If I had been able to flip the switch on my wrestling, surely I could flip the switch on my fear of Uncle Jeff?

There was one more factor that gave me cause for hope. As a five year old I had taken Jeff's words on trust, not for one minute imagining that his cruelty to me might have spoken of his own pain and insecurities. All that was different now and I knew more about the difficult past from which he had come. Now I knew a little of his story.

His mother, Grandma Russell, had passed away when he was twelve, and as his own dad – my grandpa – found solace in a bottle, Jeff's life unraveled. Grandpa remarried, choosing his drinking buddy to be his wife. She was a hard woman when sober, although maybe a little quiet and introverted. But within a few minutes of settling into her favorite stool at The Pastime Tavern she became a horrible, angry, cruel drunk. Marrying a man with similar dependency issues who also had eight children was a recipe for disaster, and Jeff received the worst of it.

Though he loved his kids, Grandpa was of the generation that never told them so. He was 74 the first time he told my dad that he loved him, and I'm not at all sure Jeff ever got to hear those words for himself. All Jeff had was the dregs of an already empty barrel.

Jeff became the object of his stepmother's rage, the symptom of all that was wrong with life. Jeff was a nuisance, Jeff was in the way, Jeff was the one keeping her from living out the rest of her days in beer-hazed happiness with the man she had just married. Jeff was the problem, and he had to go. As soon as Grandpa saw that he had to make a choice between his new bride and his youngest child, Jeff – wounded, angry, and full of pain – was sent to live with us.

Grandpa was a traditional man, the kind who valued his first-born son above all others. Because I was his first ever grandson – and the first son of his first son – I received a little of that special treatment myself. So every time Jeff looked at me, I guess he was reminded of how unfair his life was and how cruel his own father's affections were. And when he saw my dad treat me with love, it can only have made the sting of those wounds even fiercer.

Armed with all that knowledge about Jeff's insecurities and struggles – as well as my newfound belief in my own strength and resilience – I hoped things would be better between us. And when Uncle Jeff finally did walk through the door – seeing all my other uncles, aunts and cousins that had gathered to celebrate his return – and greeted me with a warm smile, I believed that my hunch was correct.

"OK then kids," he said once we had all eaten and all us cousins had decided to pester him into showing us

what treasures he had brought back from his military
service, "come with me."

Like the Pied Piper he led us out to the garden,
hauling his kit pack on his back. From out of it came
patches and insignias that he said had once been on his
uniform. There were badges and awards and with every
one that came out of the bag he told a story before
carefully handing it over as a gift to one of us.

As the gift session wore on I was OK with the fact that
I was the only one not to have been given a patch. I was
the oldest male cousin after all, far more patient and
able to wait for my prize. "And you, Dan," he finally
said with a look of mock seriousness on his face as he
reached his hand into the bag, "get this."

I knew what it was in an instant; that off-white
tangle of broken fabric that looked like a crab puppet
gone wrong. Yet still I reached to take what he was
holding out to me. And I looked in to his eyes as he
spoke. "You get this broken jockstrap, Dan, to remind
you of your broken future."

Uncle Jeff ended up staying with us for just a few
months, and though that time started with a trademark
act of cruelty, it did not continue that way. Something
had changed between us, and though I desperately
wanted to believe it was due to the fact that Jeff finally
respected me as a man, it could also be said that he had
grown bored of his teenage insults and abuses. Whatever
the reason, I was grateful for the one glimmer of genuine
warmth and compassion that he showed me in those days.

Jeff was a typical, grade A Russell: hard-working, athletic, explosive. He was a born wrestler and had competed in high school, winning a few matches by being the kind of scrappy competitor who has a lot of anger to bring to the mat. Even though he'd never managed to take it beyond local tournaments, his interest in the sport was still strong when he returned from the Army. So he started accompanying Joe, Dad, and me as we headed out the house to make it to the 3:30 practice six days a week.

I had been working hard for Coaches Sprague and Katsen for years, continually trying to better myself and address the weak areas of my game. They'd helped me to get over my initial struggles with body locks, front tilts, and arm bars, but there was one move that I seemed to have a total block against: the gut wrench.

To be fair, it's a hard move for a young kid to master. There's more to it than just grabbing someone from behind while they're on the floor and hauling them over. There's the grip to get right, the elbows to pinch in, the right positioning of the arms to exert maximum pressure on the ribs. Knees and ankles have to be just right and even your shins and head have a job to do by applying their own pressure on your opponent's legs and back. There are fakes to master, in the hope that they will cause your opponent to leave himself exposed and vulnerable, and once you're ready to begin the throw itself, you've got to have your hips, head, elbows, heels, and legs all in perfect position. Master that, and you've got yourself a couple of points and your opponent feels about as helpless as a rag doll.

I'd never managed to use it on an opponent of any
real skill. Not that I hadn't tried, you understand.
Somehow I just couldn't get it, and my opponents
always found it easy to slip away, sometimes returning
behind me to show me how it was done. Yet instead
of treating it as an opportunity to remind me what a
colossal failure I was, Uncle Jeff devoted himself to
showing me how to deliver a perfect gut wrench. For
months he tried, breaking it down to the smallest
components: a thumb placed here, an ankle angled that
way, your head lined up like this, not like that. And
slowly, despite feeling so nervous of Jeff at first, I began
to get it. He was tough and forceful and he didn't miss
an opportunity to tell me what I was doing wrong, but
he was fair and not abusive and he was giving me his
attention. I desperately wanted to perform for him, and
it was one of the few motivations strong enough to get
me to push on through with it.

These are my last memories of Uncle Jeff. Him standing beside me on the mat at USA Oregon, his tough
hand forcing my foot this way or that. The look of
peace and near-perfect happiness that fell over his face
whenever he started talking about the best times he
ever threw an opponent. The way he shouted "Attaboy!"
the day I finally managed to master the gut wrench that
had eluded me for all those years.

Even today I am not sure why he took so much time
and care with me back then. Maybe it was his way of
making things right. For me, it became another symbol
of the potential for all things to be transformed, no
matter how bleak or impossible they may seem. The gut

wrench, just like my relationship with Uncle Jeff, had always seemed beyond me, and yet with a little time and a lot of work, something changed. The move I had struggled with for so long went on to become one of my most dependable scores. I grew to love the move, and executed it consistently on Olympic and World medalists. And a part of me always thought of Uncle Jeff when I did it.

Uncle Jeff left us soon after I learned the gut wrench, and he moved on, though none of us ever knew where. For years there was little to no contact from him, just the occasional phone call and fragments of a story that described his new life as a Hell's Angel. My dad would look both sad and frustrated whenever his brother came up in conversation, and we learned not to mention him at all. And then, years later, the phone call came. Uncle Jeff was dead. The newspaper report from Nampa, Idaho was thin on details – just his name, age, and details of how he had driven his truck off Highway 45 and struck a telephone pole, dying at the scene. The report didn't include the fact that he was high on drugs at the time, but the autopsy did. His was a sad story from start to finish.

Once I'd mastered executing the gut wrench, Coach Sprague pointed out that I was still lousy at defending myself against it. So one day he had me get down on the middle of the mat and had a new guy grab my midsection, trying to turn me while I attempted to put into practice all the tiny moves and shifts in position Coach had taught me to help me escape. But it was no use, and once more I was flipped over like a steak on a grill. "Again!" Coach Sprague shouted as my sparring partner circled around behind me, ready to get to work. I failed again, and again until eventually I managed to evade it. But Coach was not done with me. "Stay there, Russell," he called, sending another wrestler in to try to turn me. "You're not done until you can evade every single wrestler's gut wrench."

I was on that mat for over three hours before I finally had been able to refuse every wrestler's attack. The skin around my torso was rubbed raw and I was bleeding. My ribs were badly bruised and I had the beginnings of a mark around my whole midsection that would last for weeks. I was hurting, but more than that I was victorious. I was learning the power that the mind can exert over the body when faced with pain.

Coach Sprague was a master coach. There was an intensity about him that I found impossible to ignore, and just the sound of his rusted voice was enough to make me want to rise up and fight to win for him. He demanded respect, not because he asked for it, but because day in, day out, year in, year out, he was there for us, patiently breaking down the minute steps that each of us had to make in order to excel. Only occasionally would he lavish praise upon his wrestlers, but we knew when he was pleased with us. For me, that came at the times when he would invite me out to demonstrate to the rest of the room. For Joe, it was the day he stopped calling him Mashed Potatoes and Gravy and gave him a new nickname: Killer.

Joe was always a more natural wrestler than me. He

could learn new techniques in a matter of minutes and perform them with ease. Not me. I was the one who had to struggle with every aspect of the sport. For Joe, wrestling was about freedom and release and being able to flow like water. For me, wrestling was a battle, a struggle that could only be won by breaking myself down again and again.

Yet both Joe and I were getting tougher and the results were starting to back it up. The local paper ran a piece about us with the headline "Wrestling brothers aim at world crowns," pointing out that between the two of us we had not lost a match the entire year, and had a combined record of 142 straight victories with 125 pins. We were getting serious about things, spending over $10,000 in the seventh grade on travel and training. Mom went out and got a job especially to pay for it all. It was an enormous amount of money for our family, but it was the price of success. And while I felt bad that Mom had to do it, inside I could not deny that it felt good to be working together as a family like this.

I was 13 and I had a clear goal: I wanted to be a Cadet World Champion that year. It was the first year I was eligible, so Joe would have to wait, but I was sure it was what I wanted. I planned my route; how I would compete at key local tournaments on the way to state. I'd have to finish top six there in order to make it on to the regional tournament, where another top six spot would get me a spot at the colossal national tournament in Lincoln, Nebraska. That would mean competing alongside nearly a thousand wrestlers drawn from all over the United States. Make it into the top six at Nationals and there would be just one final hurdle to overcome, the World Team Trials. Win them and I would represent the USA in the Cadet World Championships in Stockholm, Sweden.

Dan and Joe (grade 8) by their Olympic Challenge wall in their family room.

My training was going well and quickly led to an Oregon state championship. At the Regionals, I found myself at the top of the podium as well. Then, competing in the Nationals, I lost my first match of the year in the finals of the Greco-Roman tournament and had my second loss in the finals of the Freestyle tournament. I was second in the nation but still qualified for the World Team Trials. As long as I won one of them, I was on the plane to Sweden.

I didn't make it. I finished second in both Freestyle and Greco-Roman and had to face the pain of seeing my year's worth of dreaming and working, of pain and struggle, end in defeat. I crawled under the bleachers and cried uncontrollably for hours. I was in pain, but not physically. My aches and tears flowed from the hard truth that I was learning, a truth which Theodore Roosevelt had articulated: "Far better is it to dare mighty things, to win glorious triumphs, even though checkered by failure... than to rank with those poor spirits who neither enjoy nor suffer much, because they live in a gray twilight that knows not victory nor defeat."

I'm only 375 days older than Joe, so we always celebrated our birthdays together. It wasn't unusual for us to get a joint gift either, and in 1981, as I turned 14 and Joe became a teenager, Mom and Dad gave us a set of doctor scales, just like the ones we'd stand on before every tournament we attended. And so began a new obsession.

We started weighing ourselves every morning and every evening. We recorded our daily calorie intake and upped our training by running the three miles to and from school every day, as well as the longer runs we were completing on the way home from the after-school practices. Our dream would consume every aspect of our day, and there was no part of wrestling that Joe and I did not discuss.

At the top of my list of priorities was a desire to break through my previous year's failure and make it all the way through to the Cadet World Team. As I contemplated my lanky body, prominent ribs, and muscle-free limbs, I started to formulate a plan. I was 14 years old and I weighed just 112 pounds, but I was tall for my age. I decided that to make the World Team I would need to move down in weight. By putting myself against 90 pound opponents my height advantage would really start to show. I'd be able to use all the leverage my long, lanky build could inflict. But with three months to go before Nationals, I was setting myself a huge task. I told Mom, Dad, and Joe at dinner one night.

"That's crazy, Dan," said Mom. "You're already so skinny, what else could you possibly lose?"

"Do you know how hard it would be for you to drop that weight, son?" said Dad.

I told him I did, and made my case. "I've had to teach myself to become a good wrestler, but I'm not a natural like Joe. I've gotta take anything that I can use to my advantage. And at 90 pounds I'll be the tallest guy any of them have ever fought against. They won't know what to do with me."

The conversation went on for days, with Mom and me both refusing to pull back from our positions. Eventually, Dad gave his verdict. "I don't mind what weight class you choose to wrestle. My only concern is that whatever weight you do decide to wrestle is a commitment that you have to follow through to completion. If you decide it's 90, then so be it. But it will be the hardest thing you've ever done, and I won't let you quit. So take a day to think about it."

I didn't need a day, but I went along with the plan, and the next day the diet began. I had three months to drop 22 pounds from my already frail frame. The first two months, I stuck to a 500 calorie daily diet. It was working, getting me all the way down to 102 pounds, but with a month to go until Nationals, my weight plateaued. School was out on summer break and I decided to intensify both my diet and my training. Joe and I spent those last four weeks training from 7:30 a.m. to 7:30 p.m., with a half-hour lunch break. For a whole month I allowed myself one nutriment drink and one piece of fruit a day – that was all.

Most days I spent feeling faint and a little light-headed, but it only added to the sense that I was making myself into the wrestler I wanted to be. As I watched my skin shrink to wrap itself around my every bone, I told myself that in the same way I was grappling with my weight, I would grapple with my opponents. It was making me tougher, proving my desire to win, forging a champion, one day at a time.

Mom hated it. She worried that Social Services would step in and take me out of the home, so she made an extra effort to entice me to eat by cooking my favorite dishes every night. I knew she meant well, but it was torture. The family rule was that everyone stayed seated until the meal was over, so I had no choice but to sit at the table and watch my family eat mandarin chicken or roast beef with mashed potatoes while I tried to make my single piece of fruit feel like a feast.

Thoughts of food consumed my thinking. Lying in

my bed at night I learned how to imagine in detail what
each bite would taste like, recreating the aromas of the
meals I'd observed earlier that evening. That's when I
started sneaking down to the kitchen at night, taking
a portion of leftovers and wrapping it carefully in foil
before hiding it way up in the top corner of my closet.
I was getting anxious about food, and in the moments
that I captured my contraband and hid it away I would
feel a sense of peace and security settle on me for just a
few hours. I had food, I would tell myself; I am going to
be OK.

With the training complete, we headed for Lincoln, Nebraska. I was within reach of my goal – just a
few pounds to sweat out in the hours before the daily
weigh-ins that ran throughout the whole five days
of the tournament. That summer Lincoln was in the
middle of a record-breaking heat wave, which helped
suffocate my sweat glands and force them into sweaty
overdrive as they tried to cool my body in my tight
rubber suit. As usual, I had my sweat suit on over my
rubber suit, plus gloves, a hat, and my hooded sweatshirt over my head with the drawstrings pulled tight.

I was learning that the pain of weight cutting devel-
ops an incredible mental toughness. Water makes up
70 percent of your muscles and 75 percent of your
brain, and at 1 to 2 percent dehydration, you hurt your
athletic performance; at 6 to 7 percent, you collapse.
People die from dehydration, for unless the water
loss from sweat is replaced, the blood gets thicker
and thicker, making it harder for the body to function. Oxygen fails to get to your muscles in sufficient

quantities and the whole body starts to revolt with a riot of pain and muscle cramps in an attempt to make you stop. I learned to embrace the pain. It made me tough. I loved every minute of it.

As I was running around the Bob Devaney Sports Center, the strangest thing happened. A black stretch limo slowed as it passed me, the driver easing back to match my pace. I was focused and not going to let a little thing like this distract me, but when the window whirred down and I heard laughter coming from within, I couldn't resist a look. It was Kenny Rogers, an American singer-songwriter, who was in town for a concert. He was staring at me, pointing and laughing. I stepped up my pace and pressed on. If I'd had the energy I would have shouted, "That's right, Mr. Kenny Rogers, the gambler. I'm a wrestler. I know when to run and I'm not walking away. This is what we do!"

The tournament itself was a breeze. My plan had paid off, and no other 90 pounder was able to match me. I was taller and my leverage added a strength that was unbeatable. I made weight each day of the competition, making a mental note each time that I was one step closer to being able to dive in to the two big brown bags of perfectly wrapped leftover treats that I'd brought with me to Nationals. I was planning on gorging myself on them after the last weigh-in, and when the final morning approached, I told my dad that after the weigh-in I would head back to my room to eat there. I ran back and pulled both bags of food out. I had been dreaming of this moment. This was the reward that had kept me going through the hard times of weight cutting. I had no idea what was hidden in each foil parcel, and I didn't much care. All I knew was that I was about to reward myself for months of incredible discipline.

The first food parcel felt soft to the touch. I peeled the foil quickly and gagged. What I was staring at had a vague resemblance to Mom's peach cobbler, but the clearest thing about it was the green and white mold that had grown all over. I started crying. I checked another, but the mold looked even worse. The last month, with only a nutriment drink and a piece of fruit, had only been possible because I had dreamed of this moment where I could enjoy that feeling of being full. That plan had been taken from me. I was devastated.

Dad knocked and I let him in. There was no use hiding it from him, and he looked kindly at me as I showed him how badly my plan had worked out. "Well," he said, "it looks like you need to be taken out for breakfast." We went for pancakes, and though I tried, I couldn't finish the stack piled in front of me.

Finally feeling full for the first time in months, I gathered myself together and finished strong. My theory on cutting weight and taking advantage of my relative height was proven to be correct; I dominated the weight class and didn't have a single close match. I won both the Freestyle and Greco-Roman competitions and was the number one wrestler in my weight category. Joe had made it too, and we both set ourselves to preparing for the honor of representing the USA in the world championships in Mexico City later that year.

We were out to conquer the world. The nine days in Mexico passed by in a swirl of new sounds, smells, and sights. We got to train at the site of the Olympic Village for the 1968 Games and noticed at once how being this high up above sea level meant that the air was thin, hot, and dry – conditions I had come to welcome as ideal for my last-minute weight cutting. I watched Joe as he made steady progress to the finals – a three-way contest where the wrestler with the highest point tally would be crowned champion. Joe lost an early round against a Mexican opponent ten to nine thanks to some questionable judging by Mexican officials. He beat his next opponent, who in turn went on to beat Joe's Mexican, securing Joe the overall championship. I watched him stand at the top of the award stand with the American flag raised behind him, listening as our national anthem played. The Olympics didn't seem far away at all.

I had made it to the finals, but I had to beat a home-town favorite. My opponent was from Mexico and the crowd was clearly going to be behind him. Memories of being pushed around by Mexican immigrants in the school yard in Wilder flooded back as I stood waiting for the referee to set us to work. I looked and saw that like Joe I was up against a heavy degree of national bias in the judges as well. The gym resonated with the sound of cheers for my opponent and I remembered what it was like to feel as if the whole world was against me.

The referee blew his whistle and I attacked my opponent with everything in me. As far as I was concerned, it was Noel I was fighting, not the best wrestler in the whole of Mexico. All Noel's taunts about my Olympic dream came back to me, years of rage and pain flowing into my limbs as I charged in for the first attack, but I was immediately sent with my feet flying over my head as my opponent executed a picture-perfect throw. Controlled aggression is a great weapon, but I had charged ahead like a raging bull. I was out of control and he quickly capitalized on my mistake. He got me in another hold, and I had to fight with every trick Coach Sprague had taught me to avoid getting thrown again. Hips up, Russell. Shift the weight downward. Don't let him lift. Use those long legs and arms and set him off balance. Watch for his fake and don't be fooled.

I survived the first round but was down in points. In the thirty second pause before the second round I felt something I had not experienced for a long time: fear. Distant memories were trying to make their way back home – crowds jeering, aggressors looking at me with disdain, the pain of knowing how easy it was to give in and not fight back. I had to fight back. I had to overcome the fear and find a way back into the match.

I found my rhythm in the second round. I was controlling my aggression, looking for the weaknesses in my opponent's game. I capitalized quickly and knew that as the points inched onto my side of the board he would start cursing himself for not putting me away in the first round. I could feel his will beginning to break. And then, yes, I saw it; the look in his eyes that told me he was frustrated, that he was getting mad and losing control. This was the moment. I grabbed him, threw him to his back and pinned him.

Arriving home, Joe and I had a taste of media attention and our first glimpse of what life looked like for a world champion. There were journalists and TV crews at the airport, and more of them waiting to meet us when we got home. We were both excited, beaming like any thirteen or fourteen year old boy would be when they feel as though they've arrived in life. After the crowd of friends and press left us, I was still bouncing around the room, hands waving like a cheerleader. "Dad," I said, "when they raised the American flag behind me and played the National Anthem, that was the greatest moment of my life."

"No," he said, quietly. "It wasn't."

"What do you mean?"

"Ask me again in a couple of weeks and I'll tell you the answer."

I brought the subject up again at the end of the month. We were eating and I wanted to know what Dad had meant by what he said. "Well, son," he said, "how do you feel about becoming world champion now that there are no crowds or media?"

I thought about it for a while. "It's still neat but it's not as exciting."

"And how do you think it will feel several years from now?" he said.

I thought a little longer this time. "It will probably be just an old memory."

"Real joy is all the hard work that goes into reaching for our dream," said Dad. "Once we realize a dream we must set new goals. That's what we were made to do – to be goal seekers. That's how we find true fulfillment."

That conversation had a profound effect on me. It started me thinking about the value of the present and showed me that life is full of endings and beginnings. And Dad didn't just challenge me to set new goals and enjoy the process of working hard to achieve them; he challenged me to enjoy the journey and not get caught up in daydreams about the destination.

Chapter five
TWO QUESTIONS

The early eighties were good years for high school students. They were days of style and flair and a time when what you wore and what you listened to made a vital statement about your uniqueness. Take a look at a typical high school corridor today and it's hard to spot more than two or three different tribes represented. Back in the day when I started my freshman year just outside Portland, it was like walking into the United Nations of weird. I'll admit that most of the guys in my corridor had gone for the classic 80s mullet, parted meticulously in the middle with a little blow-dried feathering on the sides, but there were plenty of other styles. There were jocks and farm boys, metal fans and Goths. New Romantics hid behind their bangs and a handful of pop fans did all they could to dress like Madonna. Cheerleaders looked distrustfully at arty types, while guys in pristine Adidas sneakers wearing serious expressions spoke in words that few outsiders understood.

And then there was me. I was a quiet, skinny, gangly pile of bones. My brown camouflage horn-rimmed glasses with photo gray lenses that went dark the moment I stepped outside were unique. So was my hair, which – in an effort to save money – Dad always cut. It was practical and required no attention in the morning other than a bit of water patted down in an effort to tame the most rebellious tufts. My clothes still came from families in the church and second hand stores and if ever anything matched, it was a complete fluke. I had no idea what I looked like as I wore striped pants with plaid shirts, clashed bold colors against each other like cars on a NASCAR track, fusing different cuts and styles without either awareness, forethought or success.

Actually, it's not quite true that there was no forethought. I did think about what I wore. My thrift store purchase of an oversized orange and brown colored briefcase bearing the words "Laboratories Incorporated" was specifically chosen to help balance the trombone I carried in the other hand. The combined weight caused my skinny frame to stoop forward as I struggled into school, making any hairstyle as long as a mullet impractical and potentially lethal. And those photo gray lenses were not chosen because they hid the sun; I picked them because they hid me.

On the mat, Joe and I had both gone from strength to strength, following up our wins in Mexico City with successful title defenses in the summer before we started high school. Two back-to-back world titles for our age group was a major deal, like winning the Little League World Series two years in a row. We had reached the peak for our age group and entered high school as wrestling champions, but I felt anything but a champion as I staggered across campus. I had been feeling unsure of myself for weeks, and it wasn't just a bad case of nerves.

The problems had started during the summer vacation when I had been taken to get the required immunizations before the school year began. Dad read the warning label out loud after the shots. "Oh, that's interesting," he said. "It says here that one in a million people who get the shot might be at risk of becoming mentally disabled as a result." He and Joe shrugged it off and thought nothing more of it, but I just knew that this would be me. For several weeks I was unable to sleep, worrying that my mind might start slipping in the night. I became consumed by the thought of being damaged by the drugs, convinced that I was only weeks away from shutting down and being locked in my own body. I wasn't scared of becoming slow-witted or losing faculties. What I hated was the thought that, once I was confirmed as the one in a million, people would dismiss me because of my disabilities. I became desperate to show my family how much I loved them before this terrible turn of events took place.

My first period class was physical education. Joe walked into the locker rooms next to me on that first day, and as we changed I thought about the way he had changed since we had moved to Portland. Coach Sprague had long since stopped calling him Mashed Potatoes and Gravy, and Joe's excess weight had fallen from him to reveal a muscular, athletic body that he seemed fully at ease in. Though he was a year younger than me, he was stronger and faster, and as the girls all reminded me throughout my teenage years, far better looking than me. Joe was happily getting changed next to me, striking up conversations with the other boys nearby. I, on the other hand, was trying to fit both my trombone and my "Laboratories Incorporated" brief-case into a locker that was too small for either. As I banged, grunted, and stressed my way to failure, my noises attracted the unwanted attention of several of the boys.

What else were they going to do but laugh at this strangely dressed, four-eyed, klutzy freshman? "Are you retarded, man?" said one as ripples of laughter spread throughout the room. I closed my eyes and pushed harder on my briefcase.

"Hey," said Joe, standing up to defend me. "Quit that. He's my brother."

An uneasy silence fell, and I looked to see some of the guys glancing awkwardly about them. My brother must have seen it too and – typical Joe – wanted to put them at ease. He looked at me, smiled and added, "He's retarded." He meant it figuratively, but they all assumed it was literal, that I really was Joe's mentally retarded older brother. It stopped the laughing, but throughout the rest of the year almost everyone in school assumed that I was in some way less able than my smiling, easy-going younger brother.

It didn't help challenge anyone's opinion of me that the one group of people I felt comfortable around was the developmentally disabled students that were being mainstreamed into the high school. I felt safe around them and I learned a lot through these friends my freshman year. They did not hide their feelings, they always greeted me with genuine excitement and they seemed to have little to no fear of ridicule or rejection. For someone like me who had grown used to hiding behind a mask of weird fashion, tinted glasses, and wrestling, their openness was revolutionary. Besides, the fact that I had spent all summer worrying that I was about to become one of them had changed how I perceived people living with disability. I had become more compassionate and wanted to see the world through their eyes. So, at lunchtime, I would hurry over to the table where my true friends sat and relaxed as they once again accepted my awkward self. They cared about the little things like food and laughter and making fart noises with their armpits, and it seemed to me that worries about tomorrow never entered their thinking. I did not have to try to fit in or worry about what to say. I was accepted just as I was.

Starting high school meant a new challenge for my wrestling. Though I still trained with Coach Sprague in the afternoons and when the high school season was over, at school I had a new team and a new coach – Masao Miyake. He was Japanese and introduced me to a new way of working: well-ordered and fully structured with morning drills as precise and synchronized as a military parade. We all dressed the same, moved as one, and with every practice the message came across loud and clear; the team mattered more than the individual.

Coach Miyake had his work cut out when it came to me. Not only was all this team conformity new to me, but in middle school I was always going against opponents my age – now I was wrestling young men three years older than me. Though I was still in the same weight class as them, those three years made a big difference to a wrestler's strength and skill.

I thought hard as I began to plan my goals for the year, something Joe and I had done every year since third grade. Even though wrestling is a winter sport, for anyone who is serious about it, it has to be a year-round affair. That meant I was going to have nothing to do with the usual fall schedule of football games and school dances, and I was going to be heading to the wrestling room every morning before school. My plan was to take my training to the next level and reach out for the next prize. We both knew that the Olympics in 1992, 1996, and 2000 were our first priority, but to get there would require steady progress and constant fresh challenges.

We both decided that the state high school championships would be our key tournament that year. If we did well there, then perhaps it might go some way to opening doors with top NCAA coaches, and moving up the coaching food chain was vital to making it onto the US Olympic team. Qualifying as a freshman for the state wrestling championship was an ambitious target, even for a wrestler with the kind of wins that Joe and I had behind us – but neither of us had ever been afraid of ambition or the hard work it would take to get there.

My awkwardness out of the wrestling room sped up my progress within it. I shed the glasses and floral print shirts and put on my wrestling singlet and shoes like Clark Kent. I learned to find security in the fact that the team dressed alike. There on the mat my hair was as sweat-filled as the next guy's. I belonged. I fit in. But when the practice ended, the Clark Kent attire was shed, depression would wrap itself around my shoulders, and I would slink back into the shadows – hiding, afraid, and alone. And as the season kicked in and my classmates would hear my wins announced over the school intercom, I seriously believe that many of them never knew that I, Dan Russell the wrestler and that other retarded kid with the same name and the trombone were two different guys entirely.

Our goal of making it to the state tournament our freshman year was becoming a realistic pursuit. To get there we had to finish in the top three at the district tournament, which was not as easy as it sounded – thanks to Coach Sprague and others we lived in a hotbed of wrestling talent. Thanks to Coach Miyake I learned to rise up to the challenges of being part of a championship team. Still, going into it I had not lost a single match all year. I was wrestling at 126 pounds – having grown plenty in the two years since my dramatic weight loss had taken me down to 90 pounds. At 126 I was up against plenty of strong opponents, guys with big muscles that popped like fireworks, but I found that while they looked impressive off the mat, on it my technique and conditioning were more than a match for their strength and experience. Match after match I discovered that during the first round my opponent's strength would often threaten to overpower me, but as I held on and the rounds passed, my relentless attacks would start to win out. They tire easily, those big muscles, and when a guy who's stacked like a swimwear model can't take down the beanpole with the crazy look in his eyes, it's not unusual for their concentration to waver and their spirit to break. Week in, week out, my hand was getting raised, moving me one step closer to the dream.

Joe was having an equally stellar year. The Russell brothers were unbeaten going into the district championships and the newspapers started to pick up on our story. And when we left the tournament as undefeated champions who were heading to State, they couldn't get enough. We had achieved our goals without feeling as though we had really been tested.

I knew a little about state high school wrestling championships from my dad. He had won two of them himself while he was in high school, and I hoped that at some point during my four year career as a high school wrestler I would pick up at least one title for myself.

The gym was full when we turned up. Full of the same smell of disinfectant and sweat. Full of the noise of hundreds of fans all hoping for glory for their loved one. Full of wrestlers who were older than me.

I was on the bottom half of the bracket and my side of the draw was a good one. So what if I was the only freshman in my weight class, and who cared if there were no sophomores in there either? I was the clear underdog by age, but not by record, for as I read through the list of my opponents I smiled with the

knowledge that I had wrestled and beat every single
one of them at some point during the year.

Joe and I both wrestled our way through to the
semi-finals, guaranteeing our placement as all-state
wrestlers. We had already far exceeded our goal for the
year, but wanted more. I won my semi in the afternoon
but held off celebrating until Joe had won his. I had a
plan that Joe and I would do the impossible together,
that we would both be celebrating as state champions
before the end of the day.

I watched as he stepped onto the canvas, my lungs
still burning and my body still sweaty from my own last
match. Joe faced up to his opponent, the son of a great
high school coach who was a returning state champion
and senior in high school with an unbeaten record
throughout the past two seasons.

In the third round Joe tried to explode out of a hold
with a Granby roll, wheeling his legs over his head and
twisting away from this opponent, but the officials
weren't impressed and marked it against him as a two-
point near fall. For the first time that season – and by
just one point – Joe lost. His opponent went on to win
State for the second straight year, with Joe finishing
third. It was more than he had hoped for, but both of us
knew that it hurt to lose so close to the finish.

There were a few hours to kill before my final and so
we headed home to rest. But the mood at home was flat
and dejected. Even though it was not a match anyone
had expected Joe to win, his competitive nature and my

semi-final win had raised all of our expectations. This was going to be the first time I would have to deal with being alone on the big stage without my brother by my side. It didn't feel right.

I thought hard about the final, the one last match between me and the state championship. Like Joe I was up against the returning state champion, though my opponent was better known to me. Aaron Chiles and I went way back, and there had been plenty of times that he had exploited the three year age gap between us and beat me up in the wrestling room at USA Oregon. He was stronger. He was quicker. He knew the same technique as I did, only better. He had been coached in the same room and the same environment as me, only Aaron was already a blue chip athlete – recruited by teams at the college level. Aaron was one of the top wrestlers in the nation being recruited by the best schools around. There was no way I was going to win.

Wrestling is the most intensely personal and vulnerable of sports. You stand in the ring, wearing nothing but a skintight singlet that most of your peers would be far too embarrassed to wear; half-naked in front of a crowd of hundreds, even thousands and you have nowhere to hide. Your skills are matched up against another man's; your strength against his strength, your technique against his. You are exposed, alone and easily wounded, though many of the worst injuries will be hidden from view, deep within the bones and muscles beneath the skin. You can't tag someone else in, pass the ball, or tap out when you have had enough. You just have to fight until one of you is defeated. And when that happens to be you, the fact that everyone has seen you fall short makes you feel as though your opponent has taken a part of you with him.

Aaron Chiles was going to beat me. He had done it before and he was going to do it again. My heart raced as I lay on my bed and thought about that evening's match. I tried to picture myself executing some perfect technique, but the next moment I was being reminded of what it felt like to be thrown high up over someone else's head: helpless, embarrassed, terrified.

Fears like this can be toxic to the sportsperson. Once the whistle blows, adrenaline kicks in and the fear eases a little, but if you've spent your waiting time wallowing in self-despair and pity, then it's almost impossible to shake off the doubt. You tense up, shut down and under-perform and allow your mind to be distracted. If you hand over control of your thoughts to fear, you open the door to failure.

So I was trying my best to control my thoughts, knowing that ousting fear is critical to victory. I tried to harness good images of me wrestling well, reminding myself not of my opponent but of all the preparation and previous matches that had gotten me here.

I looked at the clock. I wanted to get there early and have a good warm-up, to start putting some of these nerves to use. It was time to go. I wandered downstairs. "It's time to go, Dad," I said, my voice a little shakier than usual.

He looked me in the eye. "Are you ready to become a state champ tonight, son?"

His question caught me off guard. In my moments of self-deluded grandeur I had pictured myself getting lucky and catching Aaron on his back and winning, but this was mere fantasy. There was no way I was becoming a state champ tonight. "Dad," I sighed, "I'm wrestling Aaron Chiles." It was all I could say.

Dad didn't say anything. He just smiled, spread his hands and walked past me to the bathroom. What was that all about? I had no idea, but guessed that we could talk about it in the car. A few minutes later he walked back into the room, wearing a bathrobe.

"Dad, what are you doing? We have to go!"

Dad reached out his hand to mine, and I instinctively held on. "Son, I am proud of you. Taking second place in the state championships is a great accomplishment and doing it as a freshman is even better. I want you to know that I am proud of you, but I am not going to go tonight."

"What? Why not, Dad?"

"I don't need to go, Dan. I already know how you did."

I stood there, quiet. I was trying to understand the moment. I couldn't go out and fight without Dad in my corner. I needed to be able to look into his eyes and draw on the confidence he had in me. But this was already not like any normal match; Joe was not in the finals, and that felt wrong. I started to panic; if Dad was threatening not to go, was Mom backing out too? Would I have to do this alone? I wanted to plead with Dad to come with me, but I knew that begging was no way around him. I took a deep breath, exhaled. "OK. I will win tonight."

He went to put on his suit and tie while I wondered whether he really did believe me. Did I believe me?

That night I learned the importance of the mental battle that precedes the physical. And I learned that in the midst of the high caused by the adrenal glands secreting epinephrine into the body, it's vital to focus the mind and help the body choose to fight rather than fly from the imminent confrontation.

As I warmed up, I turned my mind back to all the battles that had come before, all the training that had left me exhausted and spent as I crawled into bed. There were so many images to choose from, so many memories of the effort I had put into getting to the state final. And in the moment before I stepped onto the mat, I paused. I looked down at my feet, just inches away from the stage on which I would soon be fighting. I asked myself a simple question:

Have you given 100% in your preparation for tonight?

Yes, I have.

Are you ready to give 100% until the final whistle blows tonight?

Yes, I am.

The revelation came quickly after that. If I had given all I could to get here, and if I was prepared to give all I could before I left, then it didn't matter who I was wrestling. It didn't matter about the result. If I had given all and was giving all, then I was a champion.

It did not matter if my opponent was stronger, tougher, had more titles, more muscles or a nicer uniform. My eyes were not fixed on who I was wrestling, but how I was wrestling. I was going to give all that I could, to wrestle for every hold and throw for every second of every round. I committed to wrestle. I embraced the fight. I was wholly present for the task ahead.

I stepped into the middle of the ring. I shot a quick glance to see my dad sitting in the corner next to Coach Miyake, giving me a quick nod to show his confidence. I turned to look at my opponent. Had he grown since we last wrestled? We shook hands. The whistle blew. My commitment to giving 100% was solid and I wrestled the best match of my young career. With thousands of people watching, and the best college coaches from around the nation in attendance, I did the impossible. I won ten to four. Once my hand had been raised I raced to my corner and jumped into my dad's arms in triumph. He held me for so long but I still wished he'd never let go. Even Coach Miyake abandoned his typical

Japanese reserve and embraced me too. I grinned all through the rest of the evening, smiling so much that the next day my face ached. I guess I hadn't used those muscles much before.

The lessons learned that night forged my character as a wrestler, and I asked those two questions of myself before every single match that followed. I became a fighter who was almost impossible to beat, who embraced the fight with an inner resolve that few could match.

I had no idea how much I would need that strength in the months to come.

Chapter six

THE DEATH OF A DREAM

Once our freshman season was over, Joe and I qualified to represent the state of Oregon on a wrestling
exchange program to Germany. It was hard work, and
Joe and I were the youngest wrestlers there. But we
were getting used to going up against older, tougher
guys.

What we were not so familiar with was being
stranded in a country where we were unable to speak
the language. While we were staying in Berlin, Joe and
I had been placed with different host families. It felt
strange, the both of us being so far away from home
and separated like that.

Still, there was plenty to be excited about as we
arrived. It was our first time on European soil and
the sight of people living in sky rise apartments, the
ornate and ancient architecture, and wealth of culture
and language left us open mouthed. Knowing that East
Berlin was just a short walk but a million miles away
made it all the more special.

The first morning Joe was woken up by his smiling –
non-English-speaking – hosts, given a little breakfast
of rye bread and cheese, and walked out of the house,
down to the train station. At no point did Joe understand any of the words that came tumbling out of their
mouths, and whenever he did try to signal for them to
slow down, repeat what they had said or mime it, their
responses left him twice as confused.

Well, he thought as the couple bundled him onto a
waiting train, at least they seem nice. Perhaps we're
going to do some sightseeing together? He looked
around the carriage at the assorted commuters who
stared back impassively at him. His hosts were still
talking at him, Joe was still nodding back, and as the
train doors started to close, they put a ticket in his
hand, jumped back onto the platform and stood back,
smiling and waving.

Joe waved back, but a smile was too much. What was
going on? The train pulled out and the station swept
away. Nobody in the carriage wanted to catch his eye,
and as the journey continued Joe's confusion shifted to
concern, anxiety, and then fear. What was he going to
do? Should he get off? But where would he go?

As the train pulled in for its third stop, Joe was getting desperate. But the doors opened to reveal another
German couple standing alongside a dorky looking
guy in a tracksuit – me. I was a little confused too after
a morning of failed communication, but happy to be
reunited with my brother again.

I think of that story often these days, as I did in the months that followed the Germany trip. Seeing my brother's face shift from fear to relief in an instant as he pulled up to the platform is a perfect reminder of how much we have always needed and relied upon each other. And when life began to throw us into a series of new, strange, and unwelcome experiences, knowing that we were there for each other was about one of the only things I could hold on to.

It was Mother's Day 1984 that the dream started to come apart. Mom and Dad had just returned from a weekend away, in time for Joe and me to hand over our gifts and thank Mom for all the sacrifices she had made to care for us. I don't even remember what we said or how she replied. I just remember her looking sad and Dad looking troubled. "What's wrong?" I asked.

"Joe, Dan...we're getting a divorce," said Mom. "Your father's moving out today."

Nothing within me could have seen it coming. Mom and Dad had always been our greatest cheerleaders, the ones who were constant in their love and support of us. They were unchanging, immovable. How could they be talking about divorce?

I knew they had faced the unique challenges that young parents face when they are starting out and trying to find their own way of raising their own family, but this was not right. They were the ones who taught us how to rise above life's toughest challenges, how to make it through the darkest times. We thought our family was indestructible; Dad was a pastor and coach, Mom was supportive of all Dad's pursuits and together, the four of us were marching in step toward the Olympics. Weren't we? Wasn't that the plan?

None of our questions were answered. It was like we were back in Germany, unable to make ourselves understood. Days passed. Dad moved out. Mom buried herself in depression and hid behind locked bedroom doors. It was not until Dad sat Joe and me down that we were able to understand a little more of what had gone on. Dad had come back home to collect a few more of his things and he suggested we sit down to talk. "I owe you an explanation, boys," he started. "I've been unfaithful to your mother. I've been having an affair with another woman."

I sat there, silent. Joe sprung up, ran for the door and put as many miles as he could between him and the news. This was the way it continued to be in the weeks that followed, with Joe pouring all of his time and energy into his training while I retreated to my room and cried. I turned inward and sat with my questions and doubts. Was this my fault in some way? Had I caused it? If I'd been better, would they still be together? My black and white world where Olympic wrestling was good and pretty much everything else was bad turned in an instant to a mush of gray. My dad was the Godliest man I knew. How could he have made such a mistake? How could I continue to trust him to weave my dreams when he had done something like this?

While I struggled and lost focus, Joe's passion for wrestling intensified. He was already a good wrestler, but now he was determined to be a great one. Perhaps he thought that if he truly succeeded in wrestling it might bring the family back together. After all, wrestling had been the glue that had held us together for so many years. If he rose all the way to greatness maybe there would be a fairy tale ending in store. For a time, it looked as though he might just get his wish.

Joe and I both became state champions in our sophomore and junior years of high school, celebrating separately with Dad and Mom. Yet even though we had many of the same trophies, Joe was beginning to enjoy more success than me. Soon Joe was doing things that

were unheard of in the sport of wrestling. You need to know that most wrestlers reach their peak at about the age of thirty, yet at sixteen years old, my brother was ranked number one

Dan wins the State title his junior year.

in the nation at the high school level. Because he'd done so well he was invited to compete in the university nationals – like taking your high school football team out to challenge the best that the NCAA has to offer. He wrestled them all, won every single match and emerged as the number one ranked wrestler in the nation at the college level. He was still just sixteen.

Later that year we both went on to compete in the US Open. I finished seventh but Joe placed higher than me, taking third, and qualified for the United States Olympic Festival. There he was, a high school junior, going up against fully grown, adult wrestlers in their absolute prime. It was like taking your high school football team and going head to head with the top NFL teams. He fought, won most, lost a few and ended the year ranked number three in the nation at the Olympic level, the highest level in the sport of wrestling. He had competed against guys who were Olympians and World Team members. He had fought against National Team members and he had earned his spot as one of the best wrestlers in our nation at any level.

With fourteen years to go until he reached his prime, there just weren't enough superlatives to describe Joe's future prospects. After that summer of slaying goliaths and turning heads, lots of people were talking about Joe. Dan Gable, 1972 Olympic gold medalist and the coach with the highest winning percentage in the history of wrestling said, "Joe Russell is possibly the greatest high school wrestler in the history of the United States."

Joe Russell pinning his way to a High School National championship.

"Dan, this summer was amazing!" said Joe when he came back from Nationals. "But there was one thing missing." I couldn't understand what he was saying. How could he have done any better? "You were not there with me. This next year we both need to be at the top together."

It's humbling to see your younger brother exceed your best efforts, but I could not have been more proud of what he had achieved. And even though he had sailed past me right up to the top levels, I knew that like everything in my wrestling career, the only way of joining him would be if I was prepared to struggle and fight for it. It was a challenge I was prepared to face.

So, in the last days of the summer of 1985 we sat down and set out our goals again. Once again we planned out how we were going to rise to the highest rung of the wrestling platform together, each grabbing a pad of paper and printing across the top the title: To be the best in the world in the sport of wrestling.

Beneath that we listed the steps we wanted to take: short-term wins, tournaments we wanted to take part in, fresh goals for our training. Once they were written we did what we always did with them: took them back to our rooms and taped them to the ceiling above our beds. We wanted these goals to be the last thing we saw before closing our eyes at night and the first thing we looked for in the morning. We copied them out onto other sheets as well, putting a copy in each of our folders at school, on our bathroom mirror and everywhere else we could think of. We both knew well that, "The

making of a champion is an intense burning desire."
We wanted it more than ever.

Joe and I were never ones to keep our goals a secret.
We had always shared them with others, telling anyone
who would listen that one day we would be headed for
the Olympics. Early on in life this had proven to be an
open invitation for ridicule, but the abuse that we got
only drove the dream deeper. As we got older and our
reputation grew, goal sharing became less of a problem.
And because we would need others to buy into it and
offer their help, we called a young assistant coach, Tony
Humphries, and a teammate to come to our house one
day to talk it all through.

It was hot that day and we went for a quick six-mile
run as soon as the guys came over. We started out
together, talking about the goals with the others, but
the pace soon picked up and the conversation died
away. We ran as fast and as hard as we could, pushing
each other with every step. Joe and I were ahead, challenging each other's resolve. Could we handle the pace?
Were we ready to push ourselves that much harder?
Did we want this dream bad enough? We knew the
answers were all positive. We believed in each other
and we believed that together we could accomplish
great things.

Back at the house, we stepped in to cool down and
grab our wrestling shoes. A little water fight followed
until it was time to go to our practice. We only lived
two blocks from the high school, and since our teammate Brett had come on his brand new Interceptor

500 motorcycle he climbed on, and shouted out before starting the engine, "Whichever one of you gets on first can ride with me to school."

Joe and I both ran, but he made it ahead of me. I was left to ride in Coach Humphries' car. I remember the sound of the bike's engine as it disappeared from view. I remember listening to it moving up through the gears, thinking how good it must have felt to be sitting on the back on such a hot day.

Dan, Joe and Brett Logan

Pulling around the corner near the school we caught sight of them again. They were ahead, just making the turn into the parking lot. We saw a truck pull in from the other side and watched the bike swerve to avoid it. Our friend was new to his bike and unsure of the weight, and he banked right too sharply. The weight of the bike took over, the side of the bike hit the ground and the bike flipped.

My memories of the accident are like a series of stills. Joe wearing his blue workout shorts, hanging on to his wrestling shoes with one hand and Brett with the other. Joe not wearing a helmet. Joe falling left as the bike fell to the right. Joe's right leg pinned by the foot peg. Joe being hurled back to the right side, rolling with the bike.

We stopped and I jumped out of the car and ran. Joe's body was entwined with the bike, his leg at an impossible angle, his head covered in blood. Skin shredded.

The bike was silent beneath him.

"Dan!" Coach Humphries slapped me with all his strength and yelled, "Call the ambulance!" Instantly I switched on to the task, running to the gas station nearby, grabbing their phone and dialing 911. That done, I ran back. Coach Humphries stood still, frozen in shock. A hole the size of a baseball had been punched through the left side of Joe's skull, and through it I could see what looked like flesh pulsing its way out. I took my shirt off and wrapped it around Joe's head, hoping to stop the bleeding and push back the swelling of his brain. For the first time Joe opened his eyes – just as big and blue as ever – and looked up at me. He didn't say anything. He just looked. I held him close to me, words stumbling from my mouth: "Joe, it's going to be OK. It's going to be OK." It was more a desperate prayer of hope than a statement of fact.

When the ambulance arrived the paramedics tried to move Joe, but he became distressed. His hands flailed around, reaching out for mine. Still no sound came from him, but his eyes were screaming out to me. "We can't control his hands," said the medics. "You've got to try to calm him down."

I did what I could, talking to him, telling him that he was going to be fine. I used his name over and over and he calmed down enough to be lifted free from the bike and loaded into the ambulance. Seconds passed and it was gone. I remained on my knees on the parking lot, listening again to the sound of an engine that was taking my brother away from me. Only this time, there were sirens. I strained to hear them until I could hear them no more. I looked at myself. My clothes clung to my body, Joe's blood already starting to dry on my skin. I tried to understand what had just happened. We were on our way to practice. We had been having a water fight. Joe and I had just been sharing our goals. How could I be here, covered in my brother's blood?

Coach Humphries went to tell Mom and I ran to the school to find Dad. I ran in to the wrestling room. He looked up, saw the blood and my panic, and knew at once that he needed to run with me back out to his car. I told him what I could; that the accident had just happened, Joe was on the way to the hospital, that I thought he was still alive. Dad's reaction caught me off guard: "I always knew something like this would happen. This is my fault. This is what I deserve."

I was shocked. I couldn't find the words I needed. He was the Godliest man that I knew; someone who had made mistakes, but those mistakes did not define him. I remembered the stories I had learned in the Bible, stories my dad had taught me. There was Noah who got drunk, Moses who killed an Egyptian, Jonah who ran from God, and Peter who denied that he had ever known Jesus when he had sat and eaten with Him just hours before. Of all of them I thought of David, the murderous adulterer who was still able to serve God. In my eyes my dad didn't deserve what had happened to Joe.

Joe was in surgery when we arrived at the hospital. I remember hearing them say the kind of things that doctors always seemed to say: "We're doing everything we can do... we can't tell you anything at the moment... however, his injuries are very, very serious."

Time passed slowly. Mom, Dad, and I waited in the corner of the emergency room. Other people came and went. It was hot. I was thirsty and weak, feeling like I did when I was cutting weight. The doctors returned throughout the evening, telling us that nothing had changed yet, but somehow letting us know that Joe was in terrible danger. We heard that Brett had walked away with minor scrapes and bruises, but we began to see that Joe had little to no chance of recovery. Someone brought Mom a stack of papers to sign. They asked whether we would consider organ donation. Someone else told us that we might want to begin making funeral plans.

After what seemed like an eternity, the doctors came out of surgery. They had good news: Joe was still alive. But we weren't prepared for what they said next. "We should sit down. We need to explain exactly what happened to Joe. Your son has suffered a compound skull fracture with severe lacerations to his brain. He has a three-inch hole in the top of his head and there are fragments of his skull buried deep in the center of his brain – far too deep for us to even contemplate removing them. Between the wound in his head and the swelling after the accident, we estimate that he lost a third of a cup of his brain matter on the pavement. He should have died instantly, but somehow he's still here. Mr. and Mrs. Russell; Joe is alive, but he will never walk, talk, eat, drink or do anything normal again for the rest of his life. He will probably spend the rest of his life in a coma. And if for some reason he comes out of the coma, his body will not function beyond what you would expect of an eighteen month old baby. We're so sorry, but that is the best you can expect."

I couldn't believe what I was hearing. This was all wrong. Joe and I had plans together, big plans. We'd written them out just yesterday and had been talking about them on the run that afternoon. How could they be talking about comas and not walking or ever being able to do anything for himself again? I had never felt as confused as I did right then, never felt so conflicted, so out of step with what was going on around me. At some point it must have gotten to be too much; feeling numb was the only way I could cope.

Joe lay in the intensive care unit. When we were allowed in, we took turns sitting in the room with him. I'd stare at the equipment; the gauge that came out of his head monitoring the swelling in his brain, the ventilator filling and deflating his lungs, the monitors and IVs and beeps and hisses that were keeping him alive.

Days went by like this. Mom and I never left the hospital. Someone had brought me a change of clothes early on, but my new outfit was soon stale with the smells of our hospital vigil. The doctors had stopped bringing us bad news, but there was not much good to say either. We were delighted when they were able to take him off the ventilator, but they told us that just because Joe could breathe on his own didn't mean he was going to recover. "People don't recover from injuries this severe," they told us. All we could do was pray.

It was more peaceful in his room with the ventilator gone, but there were still times when we were not allowed in, like when the nurses were attending to him. It was at one of those times that Mom and I were waiting outside, not really saying much, when the nurse burst out of the room. She was crying. "You should come in," she said.

Joe looked just as he had before; no worse, but no better. Eyes closed, but still breathing well.

"He just spoke to me!" the nurse explained. "I was changing his IV when he whispered that he was cold!"

We both started crying, hugging and jumping up and down in celebration until we remembered that nobody had acted on Joe's request and he was probably still cold. Mom threw a blanket on him and leaned in to whisper that it was OK, to remind him that we were here with him as well.

Joe's eyes opened and he started to talk. He was confused and worried, he had no idea where he was or why he was here, and we had to explain as best we could without overwhelming him. It was like trying to pour a bucket of water through a tiny hole. Everything had to be taken slowly, nothing could be rushed. A doctor was summoned, and we tried to settle Joe, to keep him calm and comfortable and not let our excitement get to be too much.

Joe had no memories of the accident and no memories of the days leading up to it. But in an instant we knew that whatever damage had been done, it hadn't erased all of his personality as he said, "I'm hungry!"

We smiled and told him that was great, but the doctor moved in to reply fully. "Joe, because of the accident the left side of your body is completely paralyzed. You probably don't yet have the use of your throat muscles, so we're going to start feeding you by a machine."

Looking back up at him, Joe spoke. "Sir, I'm a wrestler. I will never forget how to eat!" Smiling, the doctor poured him a glass of water. "If you can drink this, we'll let you eat something."

Joe gulped it down like Rocky downing a glass full of eggs, and in the midst of the excitement, I ran out to McDonald's for a Big Mac, fries, and Coke. My brother had been dieting for a year. If he said he was hungry, there was no way I was going to let him down, even if it meant smuggling the food in without the doctors knowing.

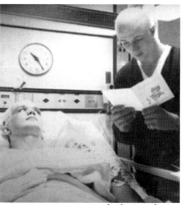

Dan visits Joe in the hospital.

Joe was alive, but the doctor was right about the left side paralysis. No matter how many days passed by, Joe was unable to move anything on that side of his body. He could do nothing but lie on the hospital bed while nurses came and attended to him, doctors monitored him and friends and family visited.

I took a newspaper in with me one day, and I sat and read to him from the front page of the sports section. There was an article about Joe and the accident. When I reached a part that described him as an invalid, I stopped. Joe was silent. I could tell that the reality of what had happened to him hit him hard. This was the moment when he finally saw the scale of both what he had lost and what he was facing.

That was the day that Joe started to face some really difficult feelings. He struggled to work out why it had happened to him. The accident was not his fault and he had so much potential in life. Why would something so unfair happen to him? Even his healing was caus-ing him pain, for a burn on his right arm – from when he was draped over the bike, his arm resting on the exhaust pipe – was starting to heal. As the scab shrunk and the skin tightened, the urge to itch it was becoming unbearable.

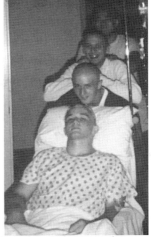

That night, alone, he shouted at his left hand, commanding it to move, but it just lay there, immobile. He was too proud to call a nurse, and what started out as frustration became exhaustion and panic. He began to cry. He was beginning to feel sorry for himself. He knew he couldn't go on much longer.

"God, I can't do this!" he cried. "This is too much for me!" All our life Dad had tried to tell us that Jesus was the best coach we could ever rely on, the

Matt White, Mike Kim and Dan see Joe Russell through his recovery.

one to whom we should always turn when we needed help. Joe needed help that night. With tears flowing, something changed. He felt as though his prayer had not just stayed in the room. Someone had heard him; God had heard him. A sense of peace and comfort settled on his wounded soul. Hope began to stir.

I walked into his room the next morning, surprised to see Joe sitting in his wheelchair, his paralyzed left arm resting on the tray in front of him, a smile as wide as a scoreboard spread across his face.

"Dan, watch!" All I could see was his right hand opening and closing rapidly.

"No," Joe said, "look at my left hand." After a few moments I saw it; his finger moved. It is hard to understand how something so simple could be so difficult, how something so small could be so exciting, but it was. It took everything within him to make that finger move, but Joe was determined to win. He practiced for hours at a time, not stopping when he had finally been able to get all of his fingers to move again; then he started work on his arm, and then his shoulder. Every day it seemed like there was something new. It wasn't long before Joe was learning to walk again.

Walking was a challenge and his left leg did not move well at all, but Joe had the will to win. There was no way he was going to use the wheelchair the hospital had given him, and he would only wear the plastic brace designed to hold his ankle when the doctors forced him to. He wanted to get back to normal as soon as possible, yet he couldn't walk. He had to learn how to balance himself again and with each step he took – first in his room, then in the corridors – he would wobble and look like he was about to fall. He'd spend all day in the rehab center, only leaving when the staff forced him out at the end of the day. He'd resume his training in the hallways, looking for other patients that were learning to walk again, challenging them to races. It didn't bother him that our grandmother walked faster than he did; Joe was determined to fight his way to healing. Just like before, if he wanted to reach the prize he knew he'd have to set a series of goals and stick to them.

He was discharged from the hospital 15 weeks after the accident. I went to pick him up in Mom's car, under strict instructions not to let on about the surprise that we had planned for him back at home. We had a great crowd of people gathered there waiting to welcome him back, but when I told him that we should drive straight home, Joe refused.

"No, I want to go somewhere else first. I want you to take me back to school."

It was his first day out and I wasn't going to argue, but it didn't make any sense to me. We pulled up where he wanted, right by the running track. Joe hauled himself from the car, refusing my offers of help. He stumbled onto the track. "Time me," he said, handing me his watch.

I watched as he took a step, then another, and one more before falling down. I went to help, but again he wanted to do it alone. He got up, stumbled forward a few more times before falling down again. His knee was cut and he was starting to sweat, but he would not stop.

"How far?" I asked, hoping it was going to be just one trip down the home straight, or at worst, a lap.

"A mile," he said.

Before the accident Joe was easily able to push out a six-minute mile. On that day that he left the hospital, I stopped the watch at 27 minutes.

"Great," he said. "Now I know what I have to work with."

The next day Joe had me take him back to the track. He was right; he had a goal, something to beat. Slowly his coordination started to improve and he was able to run a little bit better and a little bit faster. Eventually, Joe began to run in the hills around our community, day after day measuring his progress, mapping out his recovery.

By the time I sat with him in front of the amazed-looking doctor some months later, I was used to Joe getting his way. "Say that again," asked the medic.

"I want to wrestle again!"

"Joe, the answer's no. You had a compound skull fracture with severe lacerations of the brain. Your coordination's damaged beyond repair. You need to be happy that you are alive. Wrestling is out of the question."

Joe said, "No, I want to wrestle again. I know I can do it."

In some ways they were right. Joe never did wrestle again like he did before. But they were wrong too. Even though every step for Joe was an exercise in awkward, off-balance motion, he maintained his determination. Eventually they gave up trying to brush him off and told him that the only way he was ever going to even be able consider wrestling again was if he learned how to stop swinging his left arm with his left leg as he walked. That drunken sailor routine had to go.

"And to do that, you're going to have to learn how to crawl again, just like you did when you were a baby."

So he did. For hours every day Joe got down on his hands and knees and crawled like a baby from one wall to the other. Every day he visited the wrestling room, doing army crawls on his belly until it was raw, red and blistered. He had his goal in front of

Joe Russell running again after the accident.

him. He would wrestle again. He was going to find his way back to the mat. He missed his whole senior year of school and had to retake it. But no matter; it was all part of the challenge.

And me? I had a new challenge of my own. For the first time in my life I would have to be on my own when I wrestled.

Chapter seven

ALONE

It takes a long time to shake the hand of every member of your high school – even longer when not all of the 1600 students want to be greeted by the strange looking kid who dresses like it's Halloween in Harvard. But as the shock of Joe's accident eased and the reality of life without him by my side dawned, I knew that I had to find some way to help me survive at school. So I did the only thing that I knew; I set goals. I had will to win.

And I was winning. In my last year of high school the level of support I received went through the roof. I was making national news and before every big match my school announcements would rally my classmates to come out and support me: "Come and see if tonight's the night when Dan Russell keeps his winning record alive."

No longer would I walk the corridors feeling lonely and out of place. I decided that I would embrace school life the way I embraced a fight. I became student body president and got myself involved in almost every aspect of the school. I ran assemblies, dances, and meetings. I met with the principal daily. And every week I made it my personal mission to shake the hand of every other student at Gresham High School.

It wasn't just a desire for self-preservation that drove me. Something had changed inside. How could it not? For me, there was only one possible explanation for Joe's recovery; it was a miracle. Having come that close to losing him, and having prayed so hard that he wouldn't die, my belief in God had never been stronger. And the way I saw it, I owed him.

Having spent so many years experiencing the pain of loneliness, I saw it as my mission to do all I could to prevent anyone else from feeling the same way. Shaking hands was a key part of that, but so was getting a girlfriend. I wanted to show the whole school that even an outsider like me could find himself a pretty girl who thought he was great.

It took all the courage I could muster to write a note to a girl that had caught my eye at school. I posted the note on the locker with some boxes to check. One box read, "Would you be my girlfriend?" I watched from a safe distance away as the note was not instantly checked but was shared with all her girlfriends. I saw them wildly giggling and my heart sank. My past interpreted and distorted the scene in front of me as another rejection. But I was wrong. The note was returned later that day with the "girlfriend" box checked. And I instantly liked the distraction of having a girlfriend. I was elated when we were together and devastated when we split up.

Deep down, I was longing for a restored family and loneliness didn't suit me. So I set myself a goal: I would be married by the time I turned twenty. Both my dad and my brother thought that dating was a distraction, that I should stay focused on my wrestling. I wasn't so sure I agreed. And, being me, I couldn't take the simple option. I had to find a wife who was pretty and pure.

I had heard plenty of people talk about marriage over the years. After Dad left home, people from church started weighing in and giving their opinions of what had happened, and it only made things worse. I learned how to smile politely while I was raging inside as friends told me how my dad had become a sermon illustration. The preachers would tell people that because of my dad's sins, Joe and I would probably grow up to be drug-abusing homosexuals. People came over and tried to scare out the demons from within us and told us that the only way of avoiding our fate was to consider Dad to be dead to us, cutting him out of our lives completely. We refused and so we were asked to leave the church.

The pain from those days didn't slip away easily. My hurt caused me to distance myself from the people in the church and even though I started my senior year shaking the hand of everyone in school in an effort to make sure nobody felt left out, the year didn't end with me feeling quite so optimistic. Soon enough I discovered that if you try to earn God's favor through hard work, you're only ever setting yourself up for failure.

Even though my faith was leaking out of me, I never gave up on wrestling. I was still driven to win and throughout the year following Joe's accident I continued to pursue the dream. Throughout high school I was 95 and 0 with four state titles. I had invitations to visit the best wrestling universities in the nation and I had full ride offers from Iowa, Oklahoma State, Minnesota, and Stanford. My drive and intensity only increased as I saw that – just as my dad had always said – hard work pays off over a long period of time.

But, it wasn't quite the thrill I knew it could be. With every win, with every college visit, with every media interview came the painful reminder that I was doing this alone. I was sensitive to what Joe was feeling and I knew it was hard for him to watch me doing all the things that he had worked toward himself.

Joe stands with Dan on the awards platform one year after the accident.

I had offers from colleges across the country, but with Joe still recovering I chose to stay in Gresham and attend Portland State University. There were other reasons for staying as well, like the fact that I had the home phone numbers of almost every news anchor in town, all wanting me to call them with stories. Maybe it doesn't sound like much of a reason, but I've never known a time when wrestling gets a lot of press, so knowing that the local media was behind me was significant.

Maybe I was growing to like the attention. I'd felt like an outsider ever since I had started school back in Idaho, but now I had people asking for permission to come and interview me. I was becoming a part of Gresham's rich sporting history, my name being added to lists of the area's achievements. There were the Crouser brothers who did well in track and field, a state championship football program, and the fact that Portland was home to Nike – whose shoes I wore all through college. I was in the news, in the papers, and at one point the Oregonian sent a journalist to interview me repeatedly over six months, with the resulting profile winning all kinds of national awards.

Ignoring the advice of my dad, brother, and coaches, I started dating the prettiest girl in the whole school. We were great together. We were polite to our peers, respectful of authority, and never touched the parts of each other's bodies that we knew we shouldn't. I was going to do everything right, believing that God was going to give me everything I wanted. We had good, clear boundaries. The one issue that we could not resolve was faith: I went to a large Christian church while she was a devout Mormon. Each weekend we attended each other's place of worship, each one trying to win the other over to their faith. When we finally got around to talking about marriage, our relationship was doomed.

"You know, I've always wanted to get married in the Temple," my girlfriend said one afternoon.

"Well, that would never happen with me," I said.

"What, never?"

"Never."

That was it. We were done. Even though I held on to the hope that she might change, we both knew we were at an impasse. I was devastated, and somewhere in the mess of my emotions I started to really question my faith.

The end of our relationship coincided with the start of my first year of college and a knee injury that ruled me out for my whole first year of wrestling at the NCAA level. With that double disappointment came the end of my desire to be a perfect Christian. I was done with it all and I made sure I told God that. "Thanks, but no thanks," I said in what I believed would be my last ever prayer. "I'm going to do life my way from now on."

Starting at college meant starting with a new coaching team, and in Coach Marlin Grahn I found another mentor who opened my eyes to a new view of wrestling. His passion for the sport was contagious and whenever we went to a tournament he was the last to leave, always hanging around to watch the very last match play out. He eventually became the NCAA coach of the year, and he deserved it richly.

Coach Grahn was a man of integrity and I aspired to be like him. On the outside I was the real deal: still polite, still well dressed, still committed to my sport. But inside the imitation stopped. I might have looked like a champion, but I wasn't acting like one. I was staging my own anti-God rebellion. I'd given up so much and been such a good guy that in some way I started to believe God owed me. All that denial, all those years where I had resisted temptation had gotten me where? I still felt just as alone and just as empty as I ever had. No matter what I achieved, the sense of disappointment –that I was a disappointment – was impossible to shake.

I had lost the girl I loved, was nursing a blown out left knee, had witnessed Joe's accident and watched my dad walk out on the family and get removed from my home church. I didn't feel as though I could take any more.

In one area of my life I was focused and driven, which was necessary to be the best in the world. In other areas my self-discipline went AWOL. I made up my mind to show God just how mad I was at Him. I met a cute girl and slept with her. I didn't even really know her let alone love her – I just wanted to hurt God. Yet the plan didn't work out the way I hoped it would.

Instead of feeling free, I felt ashamed. I had lost my virginity with someone I had no intention of marrying, but now I felt duty-bound to marry her – or at least to live with her and be faithful and committed. As time passed, I would grow to love this girl, but not myself.

For three and half years I experienced tremendous success on the mat. At the same time, for three and a half years we stayed together, living in a relationship that was anything but disciplined. My mom and dad never knew about my living arrangement and I kept that hidden from most of my world. All that shame had to go somewhere, so I started heaping it onto her. I was always trying to fix her, to change her, to make her somehow put on a good face for the world. It was me who was wearing the mask.

I was back in the old familiar place where I felt as though life only made sense on the wrestling mat. I was grateful that there I was still able to feel like I was in control... most of the time, at least.

Wrestling's just as mental as it is physical, and I learned how to throw opponents off with my words. If I got taken down I would say, "Great take down! Nice work!" as I jogged back to the center of the mat.

I wanted them to know they took me down because they did something great, not because I made a mistake. After flipping the switch on Larry Gotcher, I never allowed an opponent to feel as though they had broken me. If I did lose, it was only because I ran out of time. I'd tell myself that all I needed was another minute, and the next match I'd explode at the start with an even greater ferocity.

Lying in bed at night in the moments before I gave in to sleep, I'd play through the day's wrestling, whether it had been in the training room or in a match. I'd visualize perfect technique and perfect position, all the time wondering how I could improve things for myself. You can never master wrestling. Perhaps that's part of the appeal for people like me; it's a sport for workers, for those who want to build something better rather than those who want to sit back and celebrate.

Because of my knee I had to redshirt my freshman year – taking the year to train but not compete in games. It meant that I would have to spend an extra year competing for Portland State, but I didn't mind about that so much.

My first time at the NCAA championships came at the end of my redshirt freshman year. I powered my way through the tournament, taking on wrestlers that were two and three years older than me just like I had in my freshman year of high school. In the NCAA final I faced Kip Kristoff, a junior and the returning champion whose dad was on the Olympic team with the Peterson brothers. Taking on the son of one of your heroes can be complicated, and Kip was a skillful wrestler who was much more experienced than me.

Kip jumped ahead of me with some early scores. It was no big deal, just what you'd expect from a guy with something to prove and the confidence to match. I kept the pressure on, kept moving toward him, kept pushing in at the same speed. He was backing up and circling around the mat, trying to stay out of my way. In boxing that kind of thing's allowed, but in wrestling if you don't engage the fight, the officials will call you and penalize you for passivity. You get one caution for the first time they spot it, then a point, then another, then on the fourth time of being called out you lose two points. Get a fifth warning and you're disqualified. Even though I had a history of pushing opponents to the point of disqualification, I'd never seen anything like this in the finals.

Yet that's what happened to Kip. Right there in the national finals, with the score tied at ten and him on the fourth warning, he backed off again and got called for passivity. He was out. It was unthinkable that a match of this importance would end this way, and Kip and his dad were both angry with the ref. In my mind it felt like a hollow victory, and it probably would have stayed that way if Kip hadn't redshirted the following year – maintaining his training but not competing in any officially sanctioned tournaments – before coming back to the NCAA finals to fight in his senior year. He made sure that he went in the same weight class as me and we met in the finals. I won eleven to one. It wasn't even close. That made it not hollow.

Success on the mat came year after year throughout college. I was a four-time NCAA Division II National Champion and was named all four years as Academic All American. I had devoted myself to my studies, and as I started to share what I had learned with my brother and my dad, my teammates began to dream too. They rose to the challenge and in my sophomore year I had the greatest moment of my collegiate career. As a team we accomplished something that nobody else has ever achieved; we had five wrestlers in five weight classes and we all won at Nationals. For every match that I fought, my dad was in my corner and my brother was cheering from the stands. Something that I thought had been taken from me forever was being restored; I was not alone.

Even though things were going well on the mat, the thrill of succeeding didn't last as long as I hoped it would. The words that my father spoke to me after my victory in Mexico came back to me.

More and more I began to feel as though I was pinned in life. I felt as though I was stuck in my relationship with my girlfriend. I wanted to be a better man, but I was just another man who was living a lie I wanted to be so much better than I was, yet I didn't know how to break free.

When you're pinned on the floor in a match, your face pressed down against the plastic-coated canvas, adrenaline becomes your friend. It blocks out any pain you may be feeling and heightens your awareness to everything that's going on. There are a hundred things you can do to get out of it, and they all begin with making yourself alert to your opponent's moves. If he has his head in your back then try to feel which way he's going to move. Move your hip up enough and you can get your arm out and be ready to push. Keep trying to bump him, to nudge him and throw him off with a rhythm that's entirely unpredictable. Wrestle to win and wrestle the moment. Remember that being pinned is not necessarily the moment of defeat.

I hated the fact that life away from the mat was nothing like that. There didn't seem to be any way out. There didn't seem to be any point in trying to change a single thing. All I wanted to do was wait until it was over.

In that respect, I guess it would be more accurate to say that in life I felt as though I was in a front headlock. When your opponent has you in one of those, forcing the back of your head up against their belly button, cutting off the flow of air to your lungs and blood to your brain, you can try to grab and elbow and force your way out, but there's really very little you can do. There's no tapping out. You just pass out.

In life, I was waiting to pass out.

But even that idea of being able to escape from my stresses was a fantasy. Life reminded me of the match I fought in college against a guy who somehow managed to bring me to the point of passing out. I saw stars, the room went silent and my vision started to go black. Three times he did it, until the ref stepped in and stopped the match. I sat on the bleachers, my legs and arms feeling like they had been pumped full of concrete. I had no energy, none at all. But the next day, after a couple of aspirin and a run, I felt fine.

Who was I kidding? It would take more than an evening of pain and a couple of pills to fix my problems.

Some old friends were back in town one weekend. They were the kind of kids who were on a mission to save the world. Good, Christian boys. Sweet kids. They wanted to meet me for lunch and I guessed that they wanted to hear some of my wrestling stories, to have me walk them through my titles and give them an update on how things were looking for the Barcelona Olympics two years away.

"We're not interested in any of that, Dan," one said. "We called you up because we want to know how you're doing. How is your relationship with God?"

Their question caught me off guard. Unearthed honest words came spilling out of my mouth.   I told them some of what I was thinking, about feeling pinned or choked or whatever. I told them about my girlfriend and how I was living a lie. I talked about my shame and how far I had strayed from the values I was raised to follow.

"You've got to end it, Dan."

It wasn't until I got home that I really thought about what they had said. Three and a half years was a long time. My girlfriend and I had grown to love and certainly to need each other. The adrenaline of our relationship wasn't something I could do without, was it? How could I have gotten myself so entangled? But the more I thought about the friends who wanted to check in on me, who didn't care about my status or my titles or my stats, the more I wanted to trust them. It felt scary, wild and dangerous, but as soon as she came home, I blurted out my half-formed speech. "I'm living a life that's not fully who I am. I don't want to have to hide and I don't want to live with all this shame."

If my love for her was true, I knew this was for the best for her too. I was not good for her. From her silence I knew she agreed. We parted as well as we could and I promised I would not date anyone until she released me. I guess I was trying to reclaim some of that ground I'd lost, trying to become the decent, honorable man again. I was sorry for the way I had treated her. I had grown to love her and I wanted her to blossom again.

My last trip to the NCAA Division II finals was in March. I did what I expected I would do and successfully defended my title for a fourth year running. I was the last Division II wrestler to be able to compete at the Division I tournament named an All-American two straight years. Brian Meehan, writer for *The Oregonian* newspaper, chronicled my senior season in a series of articles. Barcelona was coming into view and I was finally single again.

Dan Russell and Brian Meehan

READ THE ARTICLES AT
WWW.BATTLEGROUND.TV/FINISHSTRONG

I stepped off the airplane after the flight back from North Dakota State in early spring, along with my

teammates and coaches. I had my three trophies with
me; one for the national title, another for most amount
of falls in the least amount of time (won for the third
straight year) and another for outstanding wrestler
(again, for a third time). Each of us wrestlers had the
usual mountain of bags to collect – kit bags, clothes
bags, plus a whole other duffel full of weight cutting
gear: the rubber suit, the hats, gloves, sweat suits and
more, all of it unwashed and smelling like a public
health hazard – and once we had loaded up, I walked
over to the crowd of media that were waiting for
interviews.

Thirty, maybe forty minutes later, I was all done with
the press and looked around for my teammates. They'd
gone.

I slumped into a taxi and sat through the twenty
minute trip to downtown Portland. The driver recog-
nized me and wanted to talk about my fights, but I just
wanted to think about what I was going to do once I got
home. The apartment was new and I hadn't had time
to do much to the place, other than put up my trophy
wall. I'd bought four long, thick shelves and fixed them
up so you saw them as soon as you walked in the door.
Only my best trophies had made it up there – the best
state victories, the world championships from when I
was a kid, and the haul from the last three NCAAs. I was
looking forward to adding these three latest ones to
the collection, thinking about how they would balance
things out nicely.

I dusted the shelf before I started adding to it. For so

long it had been bothering me that the collection was incomplete without these senior year prizes, but at last I was at the point of being able to relax. I'd trained and fought and proved that I was the best wrestler in my class. Finally the monkey was off my back and I had the trophies to prove it.

I wasn't surprised that there were tears in my eyes as I placed the last of the awards up on the shelf. It was an emotional time. But as I called out, "This is it!" to the empty apartment, the tears kept coming.

"This is it," I called out again, only slower this time. And quieter too.

"This is it."

The sobs came faster than I could ever have imagined. I was doubled over, feeling choked and pinned and brought low by the tears and this sadness, this overwhelming sadness. I felt loneliness like you feel pain when you're struck down by the flu, with every muscle and bone seeming to ache. My friends had given up waiting for me – or had they even bothered to pause in the first place? My new apartment was empty and bleak. My girlfriend was gone and my collegiate history was about to be inked into the record books, just waiting for someone else to come along and beat it. This is it. This is all I have been working for. This is all I have.

I lay down on the floor, the carpet still holding the smells of the previous occupants. If I died now, who would care? My mom, yes. Dad, yes. And Joe too. But was that enough? It didn't feel like enough, not after all this effort and struggle.

I pressed myself lower into the carpet, the sobs coming from some deeper place now. I thought about how I had lived a lie with a girl who loved me. I felt all over again the shame that had settled deep within me. I felt disgusted with myself, appalled that I had become the kind of man who would have made the choices I managed to live. It was worse than anything my dad had done. And me with my arrogance and my talk of "I'm going to be a champion out of the ring as well as in it." I felt sick of myself.

"I'm so wrong," I called out. "I've been doing life on my own but I don't want to do it like this anymore." Who was I talking to? I knew right away. There was another broken relationship that I needed to fix. "God, I'm sorry," I prayed. "I'm sorry for everything."

Chapter eight

THE FLIGHT HOME

Carefully, slowly, I lowered myself down into the hard plastic seat by the departure gate and prayed. I needed strength and I needed help, something stronger than the Vicodin that the doctor had given when he had discharged me from the hospital that morning.

The pain in my back was unlike anything I had ever experienced – and I had a lot of experiences to compare it with. Over the years I had been concussed more times than I could count, had multiple operations on my left knee to repair torn ligaments and shattered cartilage. I'd broken my nose several times and my hip and shoulder joints were all torn from overuse. Plenty of doctors had told me that I had the body of an old man with the scar tissue to prove it. I had learned how to push my body through the pain of rapid weight loss and discovered that if you want it bad enough, it's really not too hard to keep wrestling when you've got a broken rib. And as for broken fingers, the only treatment prescribed was to tape it to another finger while waiting for the next battle to commence. Every region of my body had been hurt at some point over the 16 years, but nothing compared with the pain that was coming from my back as I made the long journey home from the Olympic trials in Albany, New York in 1992.

That's because it was broken. I hadn't believed it at first, and I'd made the doctor repeat it two, three times as he traced the blunt end of his pen across the x-rays. "Dan, you've fractured these two vertebrae, L4 and L5. I'm sorry, but your wrestling career is over. One bad move, one twist that goes wrong and it could sever your spinal cord. You'd be paralyzed for the rest of your life."

I tried not to think about it as I sat perfectly still, staring at the patterns on the carpet. All my energy was channeled into the one goal of getting through this next flight. All I wanted was to get home – to my wife.

A lot had changed in the previous year, my fifth and final year at Portland State. It had started soon after that moment with the trophies and lonely taxi ride. I worked out that living alone was not good for me, moved in with a bunch of wrestlers from the team and decided that I was done with girls. That's when I met Joy.

Leaving the wrestling room one day, some team-mates and I found ourselves walking past the gym as the girls' volleyball team was practicing. We all stared wide-eyed and slack-jawed like eight-year-old boys outside a monster truck show. These girls were something else, but number three was supreme. "You see her," I said, pointing her out as she buried a smash deep into the opposition court. "I'm going to date number three. I'll have her number by winter break."

Of course, I set out my goals and developed my plan. She didn't know me from Adam so I was starting from the bottom. Throughout September I worked on the simple Recognition Factor, getting her used to seeing me around campus. I'd say hi every time I saw her, which I made sure was at least four times a week. October called for the training to move to the Direct Contact phase, with me following up my greetings with a carefully prepared question. How's school going today? What do you think of this great weather? Don't you love the way Portland smells in the fall? It was going so well that in November I felt confident as I moved on to the third phase of the plan: The Headlock. I wanted to elongate our conversations and build up a real rapport with the girl whose name was Joy.

Still, the last day of term began and my roommates were harassing me, dissing my plan and calling into question my skills as a Smooth Operator. "You failed, Dan. You had three months and you didn't get her number."

"No guys, I'll get it by the end of the day."

I was loving living with these five guys. We had wall to wall mattresses and were saving a pile of money every month. Being with them helped keep me accountable and stopped the loneliness from setting in.

Joy (or Number Three, as I liked to call her) was about to start her morning practice so I ran to the gymnasium and got talking. When we'd worked through all the topics I had prepared on the way over, she looked at me kindly and said, "It's the end of term. Do you have any plans?"

"Not really."

"My roommates are throwing a party at my apartment. Do you want to come over? You'd be welcome."

Think, Dan. Don't rush it. Breathe. "I'm... not sure... if I can make it tonight." That's it. Keep going. "Let me take your phone number and give you a call." Attaboy!

Arriving at the wrestling room later that day I held aloft the scrap of paper with her name and number printed on it. "I did it, boys! I accomplished my goal!" They kind of got their own back at me in the four hours of practice that followed, but I didn't mind so much. I had a new goal to set.

Joy had been clear that I could invite any of my wrestling buddies over to the party, but I was equally clear in my mind that I was going solo. I was on a mission and dressed accordingly: nice slacks, nice shirt, nice geometric pattern sweater, nice hair, nice loafers, and a double helping of Drakkar Noir. I was ready.

The instant Joy opened the door to me, I knew I'd made an impression. OK, so both Joy and everyone else that I could see in the apartment behind her was wearing their sweats, but I could tell she was impressed by the way she opened her eyes wide, arched her eyebrows, and let out a little gulp of surprise. "Oh! Hey Dan. Come on in." I wasn't fazed. I knew I stood out from the crowd.

Pausing by the kitchen counter piled high with beer and wine, Joy turned to me. "Do you want a drink?"

"I'm kind of a Kool-Aid man myself," I said. Joy's face lit up.

We sat and talked and found out that we had a lot in common. We went to the same big church in Gresham. We both had a dad who had been a pastor and a mom called Marilyn and both sets of parents were going through a divorce. We were both athletes with Olympic ambitions. We were both teetotalers. We couldn't have been a more perfect fit.

She was a champion. I had watched her in the gym and I knew she was a leader. Even in her freshman year she had knocked the senior – who also happened to be the captain – off the starting line up She wasn't only beautiful, she was strong and athletic. What she had reminded me of Dad, Mom, and Joe – the will to win. She would be a great addition to the family.

I decided that since she was everything I could have ever hoped for in a wife, I would lay everything out there. I told her about my previous relationships, about my mistakes and my failings. I couldn't stand the thought of falling in love with her but keeping secrets. She didn't freak or flinch. Instead, Joy just told me about her own journey. "I'm engaged," she said.

I wasn't going to let a little thing like that put me off,

so the next day I asked her out. She said no. "You're a nice guy, Dan, and I think you'll make a great husband for someone, but just not me."

So I asked again the next day, and the day after that. For six months I put in a daily request for Joy to come out on a date with me until finally she said yes. "As long as you agree with me that this is in no way at all a date, Dan."

"I agree."

We agreed to have dinner, which I would pay for, and then see a show, which she would cover. Just as friends. Nothing more.

I picked her up in my dad's red convertible sports car. I took her to the most expensive restaurant in Portland. I handed over a gift and sat back to watch as she unwrapped the hand-painted ceramic mask I had asked a local artist to make. "Look at the back, Joy. See what I got the guy to write on it."

Joy's face was turning a little warm as she read the inscription: "First date, Joy & Dan."

I sat back and smiled. "Joy, I want you to know my intentions and I want to be clear. I don't want to date girls, I want to get married. And if you'll say yes to me, boy I'll give myself to you body and soul."

Maybe I had misjudged things a little. Joy was upset. She had ended the relationship with her fiancé but wasn't ready for what I was talking about. So I backed off. After we caught the second half of the show, I took us up to Washington Park where the whole of Portland is laid out beneath. In the car headlights with Foreigner playing "I've Been Waiting for A Girl Like You" through the open doors, we danced. I tried to repair some of the damage I'd done, telling her that I was going to give her all the time she needed to heal. I, Dan Russell, was not going to push things.

Walking her up the stairs to her apartment building at the end of the evening, just when she least expected it, I leaned in to give her a kiss. Now that was a mistake. Joy froze and it was like kissing a brick wall. I drew back to see her eyes frozen in a blend of shock and anger.

I apologized the next day. Six months later, after a lot more dates and a lot fewer mistakes by me, I told her that I was going to ask her to marry me. "Ask my dad and my coach," she said. "If they're happy, I'm in."

Her dad was good with the plan; her coach, however, not so much. I was surprised. How could one athlete not respect another athlete's desire to get exactly what he wanted, especially when he had worked so hard for it? But the coach wasn't shifting. "Absolutely not," he said. "We're trying to win a national title this year, and if you get married in December, Joy's going to spend the next three months distracted by planning a wedding. That would be the worst thing for the team and for her."

I had to think quickly. "So what if we got married now?"

"Well, as long as she doesn't tell her teammates."

I would never recommend getting married the way I did. My proposal was good enough – me covered in post-practice sweat, promising not money or comfort but love and total dedication – but planning the wedding ceremony in five days while she was away on a road trip was tricky.

I'd arranged everything I could think of by the time she came back. She returned on September 29th, 1991, and the next day she went to class, then volleyball practice, then out with her grandmother to buy a dress real quick, then to the bathroom in my dad's house to get ready. I was waiting nervously downstairs in Dad's living room when she called out, "Am I supposed to come out to music?"

Shoot! I knew I'd forgotten something. I ran into the kitchen, grabbed a little CD player and started some David Foster music. "You can come out now!"

It was magical. My brother was my best man and I stood and made my wedding vows in the living room of my dad's house. It wasn't as if our family was back together again – I knew that was never to happen – but somehow getting married like this was a moment of real healing for all of us.

Joy and I left my dad's house, arrived at our hotel after midnight, then Joy had to leave at 6 a.m. for a two week volleyball tour. Before she got back I left on a three week trip to Scandinavia. It was a rough way to start a marriage, but for the first time in my life I had found something good that I didn't need to wrestle into my life.

* * *

"We are now boarding flight TWA875 to Portland and invite any passengers who need extra assistance to board the plane to approach the gate now."

Back in the airport, I looked up to see the flight attendant approaching me. "Would you like to board now, sir?" She had a kind smile and for a moment I forgot all about the pain and the fact that life as I had dreamed it was now over.

She moved my walker a little closer to me and I pulled myself up. This flight was going to be agony. I edged down the walkway, each step sending fresh pain up my spine and churning my stomach. I was cursing the fact that the only things the doctor had given me were the painkillers and this walker. I'd asked whether there was anything else he could do, but he just shrugged and told me that the vertebrae would heal themselves in time as long as I didn't do anything stupid. I told him I didn't like the thought of spending so long in such pain.

"Well, you're just going to have to cope with the pain. You're a wrestler, aren't you?"

"I don't know," I said. "Am I?"

By the time I had made it onto the plane I was sweaty, exhausted, and even more depressed. 24 hours earlier I was an elite athlete. Now I was a cripple.

Because it was hard to thread the walker down the aisle I didn't notice the kid sitting alone in the seat up toward the front, but as the stewardess placed my bag in the overhead bin, offered to stow my walker and helped me into the seat next to him, I finally took him in.

Judging by his face he was about eight years old. But his face was about the only part of his body that made any sense to me. He had no arms and no legs, a single finger that came out of his left shoulder and a foot bearing two toes that came out of his hip. "Hi!" he said, catching my eye and smiling.

"Hey." The pain came back and I couldn't focus on him anymore. I closed my eyes, drove my head back into the headrest and exhaled. This flight was going to be worst of my life. I just wanted to get home and cry with Joy.

Some minutes after takeoff I was aware of something hitting my right arm. I opened my eyes and looked to see the kid bashing me with his head to get my attention. "Excuse me sir, I don't mean to be rude, but what is wrong with your ears?"

I smiled. "What?"

"Your ears. They're all inside out. What happened to them?"

"They're called Cauliflower Ears and lots of wrestlers like me have them. It happens when you spend too much time grappling in close with people. You get enough fluid and swelling in them and eventually the cartilage gets broken up and they end up looking like this."

"Does it hurt?"

"Not now, but it did hurt when it started out." I liked this kid. He made me forget about the pain a little.

"Oh," he said.

"I'll tell you something," I added after a pause. "When the fluid's really building up in there and the pain's really intense, you gotta get a needle and stick it in to drain the ear right down. It looks gross."

"Cool."

"Yup. It is."

I went back to closing my eyes, but soon his head was banging on my shoulder again. "Why do you need the walker?"

"I broke my back."

"Ow! That's not good. How can you still be walking though?"

"It was a little break, way down at the base of my spine. The doctors said there was nothing they could do but give me pills and a walker, and for me to rest up and let it heal."

"Oh. Who broke your back?"

For the first time since it happened, I forced myself to remember. I'd shut it out all last night and through-out the morning, but the kid wanted to know and it was nice talking to him. "I was in a match and I went to throw my opponent. I felt my back go crunch and that was it. Now I can't wrestle anymore."

"Oh. Well, maybe that's not a bad thing."

"How come?"

"I mean, if you broke your back when you were win-ning then who knows what would have happened if you had gotten beat up by some guy." He paused. "Were you any good?"

"Any good at what?"

"Wrestling. Were you a good wrestler?"

It was the first time I'd heard someone describe my wrestling career in the past tense. I wasn't quite ready for it and it caught me off guard. "I'm..." I started, then corrected myself. "I was good. These last matches were to see who was going to make it onto the US team for next year's Olympics. My whole life I've worked for this, and I didn't lose a single match, not even the one where I broke my back. I had one more match to fight – against a guy I've beaten plenty of times already – but after it happened I couldn't move. That's when they x-rayed me and told me that I'm done with wrestling."

It felt easier to say all that than I thought it would. I exhaled. My back spasmed again and the boy looked me right in the eye. "I'm sorry."

I smiled. "Thank you. What about you?"

"What about me?"

"Your, um. I mean, were you born like that?"

"Oh yeah," he said. "I was always good looking. But I had to learn how to be funny."

I laughed. We exchanged names and Cordy told me he was flying out to Portland to see some relatives. It was only then that it hit me how the really remarkable thing about him wasn't the way he looked, it was who he was. I started thinking about Joe, standing with blood dripping down his shins and sweat all over his face and back as he stood beaming on the running track at school that first day I took him home from the hospital.

"You remind me of my little brother," I said. "He was a wrestler but he had a motorbike accident. We all thought he was going to die, but he proved us all wrong. He's strong like you."

"Does he still wrestle?"

I was going to say no. I thought about how great a wrestler Joe had been, how he had been talked about and praised and beaten men almost twice his age. I thought about how easy Joe used to make it all look, how when he wrestled it was like watching ballet or listening to a great jazz musician as they owned every note on the musical scale. And I thought about how he was now – a walking miracle who had taught himself to crawl so he could get back on the mat. "You know what, he does still wrestle. He hasn't won a single match since the accident, hasn't scored even one point. But he's as happy as he ever was."

My words stuck in my throat and I felt the need to cry. I breathed deep instead and looked up to see the stewardess standing by us, two trays of food in her hands. She placed mine in front of me and paused, looking at me as if I was going to tell her what to do about Cordy's.

"Thank you, miss," he chirped. "If you can unwrap it for me that would be great."

She did as he asked and we both watched in amazement as Cordy leaned his head right down into his food and started eating. I'd never seen anyone do anything quiet so amazing, and when he stuck his head back up to pause while he was chewing, I saw that there was not one single trace of food anywhere around his mouth.

"It tastes good!" he said, flashing us both a perfect smile.

The rest of the flight I was in awe. It was my turn to pepper Cordy with questions, asking him how he got around, what life was like for him, whether he ever felt sad that he didn't have legs.

"Sad?" he said, his face scrunched as if he'd just eaten a lemon. "No. Why would I feel sad? I know people feel sorry for me, but that doesn't mean I have to be miserable. I can do everything I want to do. I'm happy. Besides," he added with a look of mock seriousness, "my ears are perfect."

I don't know how common it is for one single conversation to change the course of a man's life, but talking with Cordy changed mine. Even at the time I remember thinking I would never forget this young man or the emotions I felt. It was as though I was being rebuilt with every passing minute. Never mind that I had gotten on the plane full of self-pity and sorrow, angry that my status as an elite athlete with Olympic-sized dreams had been stolen from me in an instant. Never mind that almost two decades of hard work and sacrifice and a lifetime of dreaming had been taken away from me in an instant. I was alive. I had a beautiful wife, the use of all my limbs, and a little guy sitting right next to me who was living proof of what it meant to finish strong; making the most today of what he had been given.

The flight ended and Cordy and I sat there while the rest of the passengers filed past. Some looked and smiled, others looked away as soon as I tried to make eye contact with them. I could feel their pity for Cordy and sense their compassion, but he had no use for it. Nor did I. We were going to tackle today with tenacity and courage. That's the heart of a warrior.

Chapter nine
GOD

I was six when I preached my first sermon. Standing beside the three-foot high platform in the school gymnasium, minutes before I was due to clamber up the steps to deliver the message I had prepared, I looked out on the faces of the crowd. These people needed to hear what I had to say.

I was more than ready. Being the son of a pastor I had already spent a sizable majority of my life in church, watching my dad in action. He wasn't a shouter and he wasn't a screamer; he was a talker. He was a storyteller. Just like he did at home, he had a way of telling Bible stories that would silence the whole room.

I was wearing my Sunday suit, experiencing that familiar feeling of being held back at the shoulders, but not minding too much. I was going to be just like my dad and I was holding a Bible with what I thought was the same degree of authority as him. "Are you ready, son?" Dad asked in the dying seconds before it was time for me to speak. I nodded as a frown carved thick creases across my forehead. I had spent hours in preparation, ready to deliver it all from memory. I went through my points in my head:

   * Noah was the only good man God could find.
   * Even though people made fun of him, Noah did what God had told him to do.
   * Noah stuck to God's plans and built what God had told him to build.
   * The animals were all called by God because God loves the things he has made.

"OK then, folks." The voice coming through the PA system brought me back into the room. "Next up in our talent show we've got little old Dan Russell from right here in Wilder. Come on up, Dan."

I scrambled up the steps and strode purposefully over toward the man with the microphone. I knew the decision to preach for the talent show was an unusual one, but the way I saw it there was nothing to lose and everything to gain; I'd tell these folks some truths they needed to hear and I'd make both my dad and God happy in the process. "How old are you, sonny?"

"I'm six, sir," I said, leaning in to the microphone.

"And what talent are you going to share with us today?"

"I'm going to preach, sir."

"We've got ourselves a six year old Billy Graham, here!" he said, smiling out at the audience. "Ain't that something?"

Next thing I knew I was alone on stage. I looked out at the room full of faces. I reached for the words, but nothing came. I stood there, my mouth silent but my body and mind screaming in panic. The seconds edged by until, finally, some of the words I had prepared formed on my dry lips. "Noah called the animals in and they came in two by two. Into the ark. And there was a flood. And..."

I don't remember if someone helped me off stage or if I fled, but the sense of embarrassment stayed with me for days. My entire message had lasted less than a minute. Yet while my ego was bruised, it didn't seem to damage my faith.

I'll admit that God and I have had our ups and downs over the years. Mom and Dad's divorce didn't just damage my view of them as parents; it also challenged how I saw God. Dad had always been our leader, showing us the way to be a strong man, a good father, a loving husband, and a model Christian. Once it was clear that he had failed on one of those, I started to wonder about how I could make it through. He was devoted and passionate for the things of God. If someone like him failed, what hope was there for me?

It's not surprising that I turned my back on God in some dramatic ways when I was in college. Wasn't I a rebellion just waiting to happen? But while to some it might seem odd that I would then go back to my faith, to me it made perfect sense. When everything had turned sour and I had experienced the true hollowness of seeing my NCAA trophies lined up, it had not been all that hard to return to God. It's funny, but people make such a big deal of faith, talking about it as if it's a mystical gift or indecipherable art which those on the outside struggle to access. Or they talk about these wounds and this baggage that we carry as if there's no way any one of us could trust God when we've had so much damage inflicted on us. But that's not the way I see it. To me, faith is about letting go. It's about choosing to drop the reasons why you think Christianity is too hard, too painful, too wrong – not forgetting or ignoring them completely, but not letting them take center stage. It's about choosing to say yes to God as a coach, trusting that He knows best. It's not about denying your troubles, but putting them into perspective.

Still, it can be hard at times. When I shuffled back from the Olympic trials I faced a difficult journey ahead. Meeting Cordy was profound and life-changing in the way that it jolted me out of my self-pity, but I had a deeper, more profound problem to deal with; I didn't know what on earth I was here for.

How hard it all was came into focus one day a month or two after breaking my back. I was wedged in the back of my mother-in-law's blue Ford hatchback on a three and a half hour road trip up through Washington State. Joy and her mom were talking in the front while I was getting mad at the pillows I'd brought with me in the hope that they would ease my pain, but which were now one back twinge away from being thrown out onto the highway.

The conversation up front was loosely based on the

theme of What Dan Should Do Next. There were various ideas being suggested, but the one that came up again and again was the one I dreaded the most: working for a church. "Think about it, Dan," said Joy, turning around to face me. "All your life you've been training because you've believed you were meant to go to the Olympics, but it didn't stop there. You knew you'd be using that success to go out and talk to people about God..."

She was right. Ever since I was young, about the time that Dad covered the floor of the family room in wrestling mats and painted The Olympic Dream in letters a foot tall on the wall, I'd believed that wrestling was a tool, not the goal. I'd believed I'd been given a gift, and the best gifts always have a purpose. That's why it wasn't so hard for me to go back to my faith once I'd worked out how lonely life was when trophies are your only friends. When you've spent more than a decade believing that God has a unique plan for your life, and when those years have been filled with sacrifice, hard work, pain, and sweat – all endured to some degree because of your belief in that God-given plan – it's hard to ever really fully let go of God.

"...So even if you didn't get to the Olympics, what's to say the other part of the plan can't work? Do you think God's done with you just because you're done with wrestling?"

Joy was right. I knew it. I had been thinking about it a lot and already had a plan, although I hadn't done a whole lot of talking about it. Joy's volleyball career was meteoric; three-time first team all American, she was the captain of the national B team and had been voted Outstanding Volleyball Player of the Year by the NCAA. She'd toured Germany and the national A team was showing interest. My Olympic dream might have been over, but hers was just beginning. I had already made the transition from focusing on my goals to hers, and had been talking with the husband of one of her team-mates on the national A team who was a former punter in the NFL. We figured that he and I could just travel with our wives and book our own speaking gigs in whatever town the girls happened to be competing in. My new goal of following my wife in her career seemed like the most logical thing ever.

And yet something about it didn't quite sit right for me. As we drove I tuned out of the conversation and started up my own silent one with God.

Me: You know I can't work for a church, don't you?

Him: Uh-huh.

Me: There must be a hundred reasons why, but I'm feeling nauseous here in the back of the car right now so I'll just give you three.

Him: Go ahead.

Me: One – I grew up as a pastor's kid and you know we're the ones with all the issues around church.

Him: Go on.

Me: Two – I wasn't exactly living like a trainee pastor back when I was in college, was I?

Him: True.

Me: And three – I would really far rather prefer to clean toilets than do something like run a church.

Him: Hmmm.

I wasn't sure the conversation was going quite as I had hoped, so I tried another line.

Me: OK, well if you do want me to go and work for a church, you'd have to make it really, really clear. Clearer than anything I've ever experienced before.

Him: ...

Me: Why is it that I'm having this conversation anyway? Why do I feel like there's some kind of invitation to become a church worker? It must be to punish me. Is that right? Are you trying to punish me for my shame by sending me to work in a church? It doesn't sound like a very good idea to me. In fact, it stinks.

Though I'd gotten it all off my chest, I wasn't feeling much better about things when the drive finally ended. In fact, I was feeling worse. We had arrived at a collection of timber huts in the middle of nowhere and went straight in to the large building at the center of the site, from which we could hear the sounds of a church service in full swing. I'd known what I was letting myself in for: three days of praying and singing and listening to people preach. I just hadn't allowed myself to admit that I was actually going to take part in it.

With my walker measuring out my small steps, I made it into the room and to a chair at the back. After some talk about what we could all expect from the next few days, a guy with a guitar got up and started singing. Because everyone else had gotten to their feet and was singing with passion and I didn't want any sympathy, I made it up out of my chair, by now feeling hot and tired from the effort of getting from the car to the hall and the lack of a/c in the room.

Being surrounded by so many happy people, all singing with smiles on their faces and hands waving high in the air only made me feel worse. My back kicked off again, the muscle relaxants and painkillers starting to retreat too soon before I was due to reload my system. I must have looked as mad as I was feeling: snarling with the pain, my jaw clamped tight and my eyes burning a hole in the floor, my head still whisker short having been shaved down to the skin before the Olympic trials, my t-shirt patchy with sweat.

They hadn't even gotten through the first song when the music stopped. "I'm sorry folks," said the guy with the guitar. "But I just think that the Lord has some business he wants to attend to before we carry on."

Great, I thought. It's not enough to be tortured by all this happiness and freedom; they're going to take it slow as well. "Excuse me, sir," said the guy on the mic. Feeling curious, I looked up to check out who he was singling out, only to see him looking right at me. "That's right, you with the walker. I think you've been through some battles and you're wondering what's next. I think maybe you've been asking God some questions and He wants to tell you He heard them all. And He says you're supposed to be working for a church."

So many cries of "Hallelujah!" and "Glory!" went up, but I couldn't have felt less excited. Instead I felt mad and humiliated. How could God punish me like this? Why would He make it so I had to then spend the rest of the weekend with people coming up to me saying, "Isn't it wonderful?" and "I'll bet you're just so excited about what God's got in store for you, aren't you?" and my own personal favorite, "God must really have something special planned for you."

I wanted to tell them that no, I wasn't seeing this as something wonderful, I wasn't feeling at all excited, and God had already had something planned for me but it hadn't exactly worked out, so I was just planning on taking things nice and easy for a while. I wasn't turning my back on God, but I wasn't running into His arms either. I just wanted to grit my teeth and get through the weekend and survive the car journey home with as little discomfort as possible.

The phone was ringing as Joy and I walked through the door back home in Gresham. It was one of the pastors from our church. "I'm going to get right to it, Dan," he said. "We're starting a new church down in the south of Portland and we think you'd be great to take on the work with the young people. What do you think? Will you go and pray and talk about it with Joy?"

"Yeah," I sighed. "I'll do it."

"You'll pray and talk about it?"

"No, I mean I'll do it. I'll take the job."

There's a story in the Bible that gets rolled out every year for every Sunday school kid. It's the one about Jonah, the guy who was given a job by God but ran away. Eventually he got the message and did what he was told, only with about as little grace and enthusiasm as is humanly possible.

I was like Jonah. I agreed to do the job, but with a bad attitude. I was convinced that either this was God's punishment or it was His idea of a joke. Either way, I wasn't impressed. And yet, just like the time I chose to carry on after Coach Katsen had told me to give up on wrestling, like the time I had to convince both Dad and myself that I was ready to wrestle to win against Aaron Chiles in the state final, like the time I met Cordy on the plane and chose to battle against self-pity, I flipped the switch. Days before starting the new job, something changed within me.

Maybe I've always had an attraction for oversized challenges and slim chances of victory. They don't scare me; they excite me. The way I'm wired it's not impossible for me to do a complete 180 degree turn, to flip the switch and embrace a fight that so many of my instincts are telling me to flee from.

And as I prepared to start the new job, it struck me that maybe this wasn't God's punishment after all. Maybe Joy and her mom and the guy with the guitar were all right: God wasn't finished with me yet. And if God really was leading me down this new path toward working for a church, then He must have a good reason. If He's calling me out of wrestling, with my broken back and failed dreams, it must be for something big.

Though I was right to change my attitude, I wasn't quite so accurate with my predictions about how big God's plans were. As youth pastor I was responsible for all young people within the church who fell between 13 and 22 years of age. The potential was colossal, easily running into the hundreds given the number of young families, schools, and colleges in the area. Yet between all those who attended junior high, high school, and college, the total number of young people I was employed to work with was low. Painfully low. There were just two of them and they were the pastor's kids; they had to be there. And the real kicker was even though we tried everything we could to grow the group – from Wednesday night bowling to open invites to church and despite being constantly in the local papers – the numbers remained painfully low. They didn't grow at all. I was committed, passionate, enthusiastic, and determined, and yet I could fit my entire youth group in the trunk of my car.

When Joy received an invitation to join the national A team and move down to San Diego, it felt like things were on the move again. Surely the time working for the little church was a brief season designed to deliver a simple lesson in the need for obedience. Soon we'd be enjoying the southern California sun and thinking and dreaming again about Olympic medals and the future beyond them.

The thinking and dreaming didn't last long. Joy got pregnant and her volleyball career went on hold for an indefinite amount of time. As her belly grew, I slowly managed to get my head back into the right place for a youth worker. The prospect of having a kid of our own made me rethink how I felt about the two that made up our youth group. Would I still love and serve them if that was as big as things ever got? Did I still believe they were of value even if I wasn't getting any recognition for the size and impact of my work?

It wasn't easy, especially when Joy and I sat down to watch TV one day and saw her volleyball teammates taking part in a beach volleyball competition in Hawaii. The camera panned across the spectators and I saw plenty of familiar faces among the husbands who had made the trip as well. Shirts off, drinks in hand, they looked tanned and happy. We, meanwhile, were damp and stuck indoors in Portland. "You want to know how much they're getting paid?" Joy asked me.

"OK then," I said, wondering how much bigger her belly could get before it would start to block my view of the TV.

"$100,000 each."

It took a while to bounce back from that kind of revelation, but the more I thought about my soon-to-be family and my microscopic youth group, the better I felt. It felt a little tough and it felt a little daunting; what else could I do but embrace it?

Two years after the accident at the Olympic team trials, eighteen months after I started my new life as a youth pastor and four weeks before our first child, Ryan, was born, the phone rang. It was Mike Houck, one of the wrestling coaches at the Olympic Training Center in Colorado Springs. "Dan, I think you can make it to the next Olympics. Do you want to move out here and train?"

Dan and Coach Mike Houck

I laughed. "But the doctors have told me I'll never wrestle again. And besides, I've started this new thing now; I'm a youth pastor. This is what I'm called to do."

"Well, I hear you Dan, but I don't think your wrestling days are done. I think you need to take another run at it. The Olympic Training Center would be the perfect place to get you back on track. You need to move here and let us help you."

I was confident that he was wrong. There was no hint of excitement within me, not a single element of intrigue. Not that I wasn't flattered, but I had been on such a strange and long journey since the accident that I was convinced I was where I was meant to be, doing what I was supposed to be doing.

That wasn't how Mike saw it, and he refused to give up. "How about I send you details of five Christian organizations in the Colorado Springs area. You write to them introducing yourself, I'll add in a covering letter and pass them on for you. If you get offered a job out here, then you'll know that you're meant to be with us, right?"

I was sure he was wrong and there was no way that I was going to get any kind of offer from any of these places, so I went along with his plan and drafted a letter outlining my experience and current work situation. I didn't like the idea of letting Mike down, so I figured once I had five rejection letters in hand, he'd find it a little easier to see that this door was closed and staying that way.

When the first rejection letter informed me that I was one of 30,000 applicants and there was nothing for me at the time, I was convinced Mike was wrong and there was no future in my wrestling career. Only, that wasn't quite how it played out. I got a call some days later, not from one of the big five organizations that I'd written to, but a pastor of a Presbyterian church in

Colorado Springs. Somehow he'd gotten a copy of my letter and he wondered whether I'd mind having my name thrown in the hat as well. "Sure," I said, thinking the only thing I really knew about Presbyterian churches was that they had a reputation for taking things so seriously, they were known as the Frozen Chosen. There was no way they were going to want me.

A few telephone interviews later, I was on a plane out to see them in person. They were nice people and I liked talking with them. I felt like they were really listening as I listed all the reasons why they wouldn't want me. "I'm no good at detail, administration, or organization. I'm a Holy Roller, but if you're hoping I can bring the funny, you're wrong about that as well. When I preach I don't delve deep into the theology of the text; instead I tell stories and hope someone's going to feel inspired. And my current youth group stretches the definition of that word 'group' to its absolute limit."

When I got home, they offered me the job.

And so, for the second time in less than a year, I came face to face with the opportunity to change all my opinions and assumptions about what the next phase of life was going to look like. And just like before, I embraced the change with every ounce of strength and courage I could find within me.

With everything we needed loaded into a 14-foot U-Haul and Ryan's carry cot tied with ropes to the floor in an effort to keep him safe, we set out on our 24 hour drive southeast. Saying goodbye to both Joy's and my family back in Oregon was not easy, especially with Ryan just two months old, but both of us were convinced this was one of those adventures we couldn't say no to. And, just like before, we had a hunch it would lead to greater things. "God is opening a door to win an Olympic gold medal," I said over and over in my mind as we drove. "There's no way this is not going to happen. I'm going to win a gold medal and go tell people about God."

It had been a year since I'd last wrestled, and though I'd not turned my back on the world of wrestling and had been an assistant coach at Portland State, I needed to get back in shape and get signed off by a doctor. Thankfully, I found a doctor that was happy with the scans and x-rays, telling Coach Houck and myself that that L4 and L5 were now fully healed and as strong as ever.

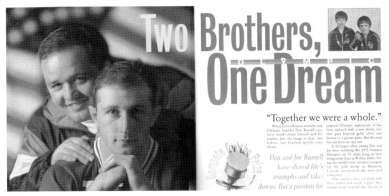

Dan and Joe were featured in New Man Magazine, 1996.

If you go to Colorado Springs today you won't be able to miss the Olympic rings all around the US Olympic Training Center. Like a university campus, the walls of the USOTC offer constant reminders of the future that awaits those who are prepared to invest enough of themselves in the present. Photos of past champions, Olympic torches in display cabinets, equipment from record breaking sporting feats are all on display, all colliding to fill the atmosphere with a sense of purpose and promise.

There were less than a thousand days to go before the next Olympic games began. This was the era of Carl Lewis and the Dream Team, and hopes were high for an exceptional US medal haul as the 1996 games came to Atlanta. I was aware of how much work was needed, and as I walked into the newly built wrestling room for the first time, I looked at what Coach Anatoly Petrosyan had pinned up. It was a list of every practice that lay ahead of us, not only covering the techniques we would drill but the level of intensity at which we would be training. When we were months away from major competitions the training would be long and low intensity, but the closer the big meets got the shorter and more intense our work would become. Also on the wall were the details of doctors, dietitians, and sports psychologists who were available to us whenever we wanted. I had never been in a room that felt so well prepared for success.

The smell of the room, however, was like every other wrestling room I had trained in: sweat and plastic-coated mats. The sound of dull thuds as bodies hit the mat beat out the rhythm I had been moving to since just after I could walk. The shouts of the coaches, of wrestlers psyching themselves up, of opponents calling out to tease each other. I wanted this, I grabbed hold of it. I was home again, back in the one place that had presented me with challenges I could overcome, with problems I could work through and people I could learn from. There was no sign of the mantra Coach Sprague had made us repeat before every practice, but I knew the words so well that I said them automatically as I jumped onto the mat. If the making of a champion was an intense burning desire, then I wanted to be on fire.

The work at the church was a perfect accompaniment to training, which started out well and got better and better. Each day, morning and evening, I'd take myself to the wrestling room. I'd look around at the other guys in the room and know that I had already competed against everyone in my weight class, as well as plenty of the ones who were one and two classes heavier. These were the best wrestlers in the country – as well as the occasional visitor from overseas who came along to join in and spar with us. If ever I believed that I was going to win at the Olympics, it was now.

Every Thursday at the USOTC, Olympic Champion and Coach Steve Fraser introduced us to a training regime that shaped him into a gold medalist. I often dreaded Thursdays, but I loved them too. They were the day of the Grind Match – the time when champions were forged. If you have ever wrestled, you know how tired you become and how quickly the fatigue sets in. Even spectating at a high school match can reveal this, as you watch young, energetic men hardly able to stand after just six minutes of wrestling. A six minute match is nothing compared to the Grind Match.

On Grind Match days we were paired off with a team-mate that was of the same skill level and size. Over the next two hours our job was to break our opponent

Dan ices his shoulder after a Grind Match.

mentally, physically, and emotionally as often as possible. We wrestled without any breaks, without any water, without any out of bounds area on the mat. We did anything we could to totally dominate our opponent and it took everything in me not to be broken myself. My mind and my body would scream to quit. My lungs would burn as I felt as though I couldn't get enough oxygen. My arms and legs became like dead weights, but I couldn't give up. My opponent kept coming at me and we spent every one of the 120 minutes pushing, swinging our arms, mauling each other. "Which one of you is going to quit first?" the coaches would shout. And every Thursday at least one of the best wrestlers in the world would run out of the room, kicking over gar-bage cans, screaming in agony. He had been broken and he could not continue anymore. Because I often wres-tled against men that were bigger and stronger than me in tournaments, I knew that I could not be broken. I just needed to wait for my time to strike. I learned to be patient. I learned to wear my opponent down. I learned that to be the conqueror, I needed to finish strong.

The first overseas trip took me to Sweden to compete in the Haparanda Cup, right up in the north on the border with Finland. It was cold and dark most of the day, but in this little community I found a fresh sense of excitement as I prepared to put my body and will up for its first test since the accident. I made it through to the final where I faced Törbjorn Kornbak. He was a local guy, but a rock star in Sweden. He was an Olympic and World medalist, a tall, blond, muscled Viking warrior. You could even go into the post office and buy a stamp with his face on it. His fans made more noise than any I'd ever heard as we waited for the referee to blow the whistle and our battle to commence.

I've always known that any overseas match starts with you three points down, so it didn't bother me that the first few calls went against me. I stayed present, never stopped moving forward, and got myself in a position to carry out a perfect throw. It was a beautiful thing: my hips in, his head down and his little Viking feet sailing through the air like a pair of seagulls. Somehow they scored it for him; a terrible call that made no sense at all. The match drew to a close and still I out-wrestled him, but the bias was too much to overcome and I lost seven to six.

"Coach!" I shouted excitedly as I left the mat. "I'm back, coach! I can wrestle at this level!"

Coach Houck grabbed me by the singlet and forced me back against the wall, his elbow across my throat, his eyes stabbing at mine. "How can you be so satisfied, Russell? You lost! You've got to find a way to win. You have to win."

Coach Houck was right, I did need to find a way to win, but not just in wrestling. I needed to learn how to let my faith be my ultimate source of strength.

After Sweden I traveled a lot more, constantly searching out the best opponents in the world to help my preparation for Olympic glory. I went to Cuba, to Turkey, Italy, Hungary, France, Finland, Norway, and beyond. As Atlanta '96 approached I had wrestled in 42 different nations.

It was on one of those trips I found myself awake at 2 a.m. in Veliko Tarnovo, the Old Bulgarian capital. The best teams in the world had gathered for a competition, and I had found it particularly hard to sweat out the pounds in time for the weigh-in the night before competing. I had gone on several long runs trying to cut weight, and on one of the runs I had taken a quick detour into a local market and bought a big bottle of grape juice. I finished my run with the full bottle in one hand, looking forward to opening it after the weigh-in.

Later that evening our team physician told me he was concerned about the dark yellowness in my eyes, telling me I was too dehydrated for his liking. I went to the hospital, was checked out and hooked up to an IV for an hour or two.

By the time 2 a.m. came around I was feeling ill. My tongue felt sticky and swollen and as I started feeling around in my bag for the grape juice, my roommate,

Isaac, spoke up. "Can't sleep either, huh?"

"No," I replied. "I'm still feeling dehydrated." I turned on the light, found the bottle and opened it up. It felt so good. Isaac pulled out some bread he had bought from the local bakery and the two of us sat there, feasting while the rest of the hotel slept.

"This is a great combination," I said, throwing back more juice and bread. "I can't remember when something tasted this good."

"You know why, don't you?" Isaac asked.

"No. Tell me."

"This is communion, right? Bread and grape juice."

Both of us fell silent for a minute.

When the quiet passed, we spoke about how this was a great moment to actually take communion together, to remember the sacrifice of Jesus. We had both experienced the pain and sacrifice of weight cutting that day, but nothing compared to the sacrifice that Jesus made when he decided to die for us.

Because of that nighttime communion, something changed in me. Thoughts of sacrifice, pain, and purpose took on a whole new meaning. I wrestled the next day and made it on to the podium for a medal, but it was about more than that one single victory. As I traveled I began to notice more and more the way God was at work. In Israel I met some of the toughest wrestlers I'd ever encountered, men who were hungry for more than the medals and the glory. Our own heavyweight was Jewish and as soon as the competition was over, he asked me if I would go with him to the Wailing Wall.

David was a grown man who had never had a bar mitzvah, but something about being at the foot of the ancient temple stirred him. I walked with him as he went searching for a rabbi who would lead him on this rite of passage. The rabbi led us into the tunnel near the wall and spoke a beautiful blessing over my friend and teammate. "What is the meaning to life?" the rabbi translated at one point. "The mitzvah reminds us of the beauty that is to be found in pursuing closeness to God."

Dan and David Koplovitz at the Wailing Wall.

Dan Russell was sponsored by Nike in pursuit of his Olympic Dreams. In
one of Nike's most iconic wrestling ad campaigns, "Wimps need not apply."
Dan throws teammate and All-American Eric Winters.

Dan is featured in this famous 'blender' ad throwing future rival Matt Lindland.

Chapter ten

ONE LAST MATCH

A lot of people try to compare wrestling to boxing. They think because of the nature of the physical contact and the style of our training, we wrestlers must be like boxers. If you ask me, it's a good comparison, but not the best. The sportspeople that guys like me have the most in common with are long distance runners. We share the same mental scars.

There's a point in the run where your body gets your brain to do the dirty work and tell you that it's done. No more. You've pushed me too hard. I'm packing up here. And that's the exact point at which the runner and the wrestler alike find the strength to ignore the threats of collapse and the attacks of muscle cramps and burning lungs and keep pushing on.

I did a lot of running when I was wrestling. Partly it helped with the weight loss, but more than that it gave me the opportunity to do battle with myself and win. It wasn't enough to rack up ten or fifteen miles after evening practice; I'd invent challenges within the run to make things even harder. If I made it to the next telephone pole before three cars passed me then I would have won. Make it to the next pole before I saw a bird overhead and I'd be a champion. I was constantly competing, always pushing myself against the elements, always forcing myself to the point at which I was desperate to stop and then still further. I hated it and I loved it too.

The differences between running and wrestling are obvious. While the run will throw wind, rain, the occasional stray dog and the odd careless driver at you, on the wrestling mat there's a man who is trying to use his full strength and speed to bring you down. Trying to keep alert, to resist the attacks and fight back when your body is beyond the point of exhaustion forces you to dig deep, which is why so many wrestlers end up going through special forces training.

While the individual gets honored and celebrated in other sports, even in team sports like football and basketball, wrestling is always about more than the man on the mat. Wrestling has such a strong sense of national identity and it's a great honor to be able to wrestle for the place you come from. To see your flag raised and hear your anthem sung is to realize that you're wrestling for something far greater than yourself. You're wrestling for God, the pride of your country, for your family and community and everyone else back home.

All of this was in my mind as I traveled back from the Haparanda Cup in Sweden and prepared to enter my final year before the '96 Atlanta games. I knew what was at stake, and I was determined to add to the US medal haul and play my part in boosting the profile of wrestling within the US. I was prepared to give more in my practices than I had ever given before. I had been given a fresh chance where there should have been none. There was no way I was going to waste it.

The first challenge was to make it onto the US wrestling team, and that meant finishing well in the mid-year ranking tournament. Everything was going well until I hit the semi-finals. I had been drawn against Matt Lindland, a hard working teammate I knew well. He'd been my training partner in the past and I'd taught him everything I knew – about being present, about working to break your opponent, about committing to the fight and saying yes to the intensive preparation that marks every good fighter out from the crowd.

Matt was tough to fight. He, more than anyone I knew, had learned how to embrace the fight. Even though I was beating him as expected, he was refusing to give up. I pushed against him, trying to throw him off his guard, but there was no sense that he was going to be broken. There were clearly no shortcuts to beating him.

At some point in the final he was getting frustrated and was down on points. I continued my push but Matt caught me off guard, snapped my head down, and got me in a front headlock. I had spent many hours working on defending a strong front headlock and because this was my favorite offensive move to put on someone, I understood exactly where my neck and shoulders would need to be in order to not be turned. I moved my head from one side of his body to the other and worked hard to get my hips under me and my head up. My defense was working and Matt was not able to score, which only caused his frustration level to increase further. As the official moved to the other side of us I found Matt's finger hooking into my mouth and twisting inside my cheek. He fishhooked me hard, yanking my cheek away with such force that I thought my face was going to come off. It was illegal, underhanded, and completely out of sight of the officials, so he got away with it. Even though I won the match and Matt failed to score, what he did stayed with me. It left me feeling something I was not used to feeling: dishonored and disrespected. Perhaps if it was anyone else who had done it to me I would not have felt the same way, but Matt was special. I had trained him, taken him under my wing. We had grown up in the same club program, both under the gaze of Coach Sprague and Coach Katsen and both of us were now under Coach Petrosyan. We had a life out of the wrestling room as well, and we had talked about God and what it means to be a Christian. We'd prayed together, and yet he still chose to try to break me with a cheap, illegal move?

I knew that getting angry is where we make our biggest mistakes. When we allow our emotions to take over, we give in to uncontrolled aggression and invite our opponent to score against us. Instead it's important to have controlled aggression, to work to win the moment, stay present, forget what just happened, forget about what might happen. Stay disciplined. That's what I had to do in the finals, where I faced Darrell Gholar.

Darrell had arms three times the size of mine and legs that were even bigger. He was explosive and had sat at the top of the US rankings for many years. I never had a problem against guys like him for the bigger they looked, the more easily I knew they would tire. Because I had worked so hard on my fitness I was able to continue to wrestle at full pace throughout the whole match. To the opponent with big, explosive muscles it felt as though I was getting stronger.

That's what happened with Darrell as I pushed him to the end of the match, eventually winning three to nothing. It wasn't a big score, but it told the story clear enough; I had wrestled him to the end, refusing to allow him to use his power against me. I was ranked number one in the US and set off to Russia to compete in my second ever Poddubny tournament.

It was the perfect preparation for my trip to Russia. Not only was I fighting well, I was fighting with heart. I was ready to fight for the honor of my country and had never felt more proud to be an American wrestler. I went to Poddubny hungry to test myself against the best and found that my dreams and hunches were not so far from reality after all. As I sat and listened to the deep Russian growls of affirmation and encouragement given to me at the post-tournament banquet, I knew I was on the home stretch of my race to the Olympics. And as my final opponent Totlak and I hung out in my room after the feast, laughing and joking, trading my Levis for his "shopka," a Russian fur hat, the possibility of my plan not working out never even entered my mind.

A year before the Atlanta Games, the city was host to the World Team Trials. It was a chance for the organizers to make sure that the Games themselves were going to run well, and for those of us competing it was an opportunity to take our preparations to a whole new level.

I was up against Gordy Morgan, the guy I'd been wrestling when I'd broken my back in the trials for the Barcelona 1992 Games. When we met in Atlanta he was wrestling well and got himself in a position where he could throw me: both my arms trapped to my sides and my whole body lifted off the mat. To stop it I knew I had to make myself as long and awkwardly shaped as possible, so I posted, stretching my neck out as far forward and my legs as far back as I could. It worked a little, but Gordy still managed to get the throw in.

Being thrown is a fearful experience. It's the reason why you do a lot of tumbling while you are training, so you can learn how to fall correctly and reduce the risk of serious head and neck trauma. But injuries happen. They're all part of the deal. As my body sailed up and over Gordy's chest, I could feel my gravity taking a hold on me, my feet lifting high and my head coming down fast toward the mat.

After that, my memory is blank. There are vague thoughts about lying on the mat and having lights shone in my eyes, but they might just be memories I've created from the stories people told me. What I do remember is the hospital, but even then my memories are hazy. Apparently I lost about six years of my life, so

I had no knowledge of Ryan, Joy, or breaking my back four years earlier. I was under 24 hour care and not allowed to sleep more than thirty minutes at a time, for fear that my brain may decide being conscious was far too much work and ease me gently into a coma. I do remember the sense of panic that flowed through me and the series of questions I asked every one of my teammates who visited:

"Where am I?"

"What happened?"

"Am I going to wrestle again?"

At first they gave me the straight answers:

"You're in the hospital."

"You got thrown, landed on your head and were concussed."

"Yeah, you'll be fine, Dan."

Once we'd reach that point in the conversation I'd look away, tune out for a few seconds then start all over again: "Where am I?"

Apparently the guys got a little tired of all this and wanted to have some fun, so they started making up increasingly elaborate answers, telling me we were in Atlanta – showing me the hospital logo to prove it – and that I had been injured in the Olympic finals. "But you won, Dan. You won gold!"

"Really?" I said, before the pause and brief look out the window. Then, "Where am I?"

Still, within a week I had recovered enough to regain all my memory, get discharged, and be allowed back to training.

It wasn't the only time I spent in the hospital during my career. I'd had surgeries and other injuries that had needed to be checked out, and I'd known many other wrestlers who had suffered far worse than I had. Back in high school a friend got thrown during a match and landed badly. I went to see him in the hospital hoping I could help inspire him to work on his recovery just like Joe had, but I was wrong. Recovery wasn't an option.

"I can't move from the neck down," he told me, but not with any sense of self-pity or anger toward the guy who had thrown him. In fact, what he wanted more than anything was to watch the tape of the fight and have me replay the throw again and again. "Wow," he'd say as we watched the last seconds of his life as he had known it, "look at the explosion of his hips. That was a beautiful throw, wasn't it?"

Wrestlers aren't like normal people, and there's a lot to be celebrated about the way we embrace the struggles of life. We don't worry about feelings and we're not going to let something as petty as pain or even paralysis stop us from setting goals and moving on with our lives. But we can be stupid and stubborn and too much in our own heads to notice the world around us.

I was reminded of this a few weeks after getting back from Atlanta. I was wrestling well, committing my all to the practices and meeting all my training targets. I was goofing around with one of the guys a couple of weight classes heavier than me and he had me in a reverse head lift, carrying me upside down around the room while the other guys laughed. I heard the doors to the room open and felt his grip on my torso tighten. I looked and, though upside-down, made out the figure of one of this guy's key opponents. A red mist must have settled on my buddy, for I felt myself being lifted high for a fraction of a second, then he pile-drove me right into the mat, straight down, head first. Again, for the second time in a few months, I was out cold. Yet again, I woke up in the hospital, feeling confused and concerned.

I recovered again, but the injuries kept coming. Four weeks before the trials that would decide which wrestlers would make it onto Team USA, I went for a throw against a cat-like opponent with quick reflexes. I knew I would have to throw him with every ounce of strength I could muster. The throw was perfect. My opponent was unable to twist out of the move and flew from his feet to his back. In the middle of the throw I felt a fierce pain erupt along the left side of my ribcage. For the pain to break through the anesthesia of adrenaline told me something straight away; this was not good.

I went, as I always did, to see the team doctor, Dr. Bernie Feldman. Bernie was a trauma doctor for a

major hospital in Chicago, but he also served as one
of the main doctors the team used whenever there
was a major tournament. Bernie and I went back, and
I trusted him. In the past he'd stitched up my eye in
between rounds and then sent me back out. He had
been with me at the Poddubny, but more importantly
he'd been there when I broke my back in '91, as well as
when I had been concussed both in Atlanta and back
at the USOTC. He knew me, he knew my body, and he
knew how important it was that I make it through to
the trials in one piece.

"Well," he said, "It looks like you broke your ribs
and you've torn a fistful of muscles that you really are
going to need when you next want to throw a guy. So
you can't wrestle until the trials. And even then, you're
going to need some cortisone shots to numb the pain."

There was nothing I could do but accept what he
said and commit to full training, but no wrestling until
the team trials just outside San Francisco. I took to
the hiking trails outside Colorado Springs and bested
myself on the track that climbs 2,000 feet in less than
a mile. My legs always ended up feeling like dead tree
stumps, and I hoped the pain was enough to keep me in
shape before the trials.

From the start everything was wrong. There was a
problem with the original venue and they had to make
a last minute change, so we ended up wrestling in a
place that made everything about the trials harder.
There was no air conditioning yet the summer was in
full force outside. The venue was dirty, the wrestling

mat was elevated on a stage in the middle of the room, and the whole thing felt a long, long way from Atlanta. And yet, this was it; the last hurdle to overcome. The number one wrestler in each weight class would be going to the Olympics. Everyone else would be a spectator.

Despite the problems with the logistics, I was focused. I was there with a single aim in mind: to overcome the final obstacle before my Olympic dream finally came into view. Everybody knew it and there was a sense of fairytale ending in the making as I looked around the hall. Dad and Joe were my coaches, so they were in my corner for all my matches. Mom and Joy and even my Grandpa were there too, and there must have been about fifty people from up in Portland who had made the nine hour drive south. They were all wearing fluorescent pink t-shirts that had "Team Dan" written across the back in bold, black letters. It was easy to spot them from anywhere in the room, and I liked the idea that these people who had walked with me through so many obstacles and sat through so many matches were about to see me win one of my most significant tournaments of my career.

And yet, something wasn't right. I started slow and lost my first match. It wasn't a disaster – there were enough matches ahead for me to pull back – but I knew I wasn't competing at the level required of an Olympic champion. I was nowhere close to my best and that left me feeling frustrated and discouraged.

Before the next match started, I noticed my thoughts

were drifting. I felt unsettled, maybe even unsure. It was strange to feel this way, but all I had to do was remind myself of who my opponent was to understand why. It was Matt Lindland, the guy who I had mentored, trained, and kept under my wing for so long. The only guy who I felt I had never truly broken.

The match started and I was soon up one to nothing, but it didn't feel like winning. I started to worry about the outcome, to let my thoughts drift away from the fight toward the frustration and the pain that came with my injured ribs. Though I'd had a cortisone shot before the match began, the injury was never far from the front of my mind. And Matt – well, he fought just like he had before, embracing the fight but doing little extra things that are right on the edge of being legal; no fishhooks, but a few head-butts and thrown elbows here and there. I let fear creep in to my thoughts and I started whining and complaining, trying to get the officials on my side, pointing out all that Matt was doing. All I ended up doing was showing him how well his strategy was working.

Distracted and annoyed, I was failing on so many levels. I was not finding a way to win, not embracing the fight, not wrestling the moment. And when he sucker-punched me in the left side, right where I had injured myself in my last match, I let the pain get the better of me. I was winded and needed time to force my chest muscles to relax and allow my breathing to settle again. I needed to get my head and thoughts right. I pulled back, signaled to the ref for time out and, as he blew the whistle to show that the fight was on pause, I turned to walk back to my corner.

I had never turned my back on a wrestler during a fight before, not even when a time out had been called. And I would never do it again. Holding my left side and trying to recover my breath as I took small steps away from the fight, I felt Matt's arm's reach around my torso and pull me back. My arms were trapped and I was off my feet. He swung me back around to the center of the mat, threw his hips in, leaned back and hauled me back over his body, my feet tracing a perfect semi-circle in the air like a rainbow.

It was a beautiful throw.

The mat was on a platform elevated four feet above the floor. It meant that it was easier for spectators to see but further for me to fall. My head hit the ground first, though it was not the soft canvas of the mat that broke my fall, but the hard wooden floor that surrounded the elevated stage.

I could hear Mom shouting, calling someone a "sonnofabitch!" I could sense that Joy was near. Dad's voice was close too. And the light was back, moving from side to side, taking up my whole field of vision. Then a voice that I knew well, a voice that always came with the light: "He's done."

Bernie had me taken out from the gym and laid me on a massage table in the back, where I started to come back around. Mom was enraged and Joy had tears in her eyes. Bernie looked concerned.

It took a while for the details of the fight to come back to me, but this was nothing like the Atlanta concussion. Instead of fear and confusion, a sadness had taken up residence within me. I didn't talk much as the hours passed, but I was thinking at a hundred miles an hour. Why had I let Matt get to me like that? Why had I turned my back on him? Did I really trust him not to chase after me, or did I in some way want him to? Did Matt know the only way he could beat me was by playing dirty? Did he hear the whistle and attack anyway, or had he just been so in the moment, so present to the fight that he hadn't heard the ref's call? Inside, my thoughts were toxic. I wanted Lindland to get what he deserved, but perhaps I was the one who was getting what he deserved.

"It's OK, Dan," said Mom. "I'm sure Lindland's going to be disqualified for what he did to you."

I remember her words sounded very small in the room. And the longer the silence that followed them, the smaller they got. It was Bernie who spoke next.

"Dan, even if they disqualify Matt for what he did, you know the risks; three major concussions like yours spread across a whole lifetime is enough to limit your brain capacity drastically when you hit fifty. But this is your third major concussion in less than a year. Your wrestling career is done."

Unlike Mom's words, Bernie's just seemed to get bigger as the silence fell on the room. "Dan," he continued, "I can't let you wrestle any more. You're done for good this time."

In the days that followed I felt fine. The family that had driven to join us had no appetite at all for sitting in a gym watching other wrestlers get excited about going to the Olympics, so we all blew it off and went to downtown San Francisco. We laughed about how, as I lay on the massage table, things had gotten so ugly out in the gym, with my family in their matching pink t-shirts all pressing in on the officials and shouting down Matt Lindland and his team. The security guards had gotten so stressed that they had been heard saying, "What are we going to do with the pink family?" before pushing all fifty of them out of the door and onto the street. I heard Dad had been there too, and that Joe had used all his force to hold him back.

I knew it was over, but I hadn't let the truth of it sink in. It was only when I caught Mom crying when she thought I wasn't looking that I realized the pain of what had happened. "I'm sorry Dan," she sniffed. "But I just feel bad that it had to end like that. It was your last match and at the end of your last match you're supposed to walk out, leave your shoes on the mat, and listen to people applaud you. You just got carried out on a gurney."

It was too much for me too, but it wasn't like the previous Olympic trials. There I had been full of self-pity from the get-go, but this time it was the questions that troubled me straight away. Why would God have me move my wife and now two children away from their grandparents and parents, away from the community, for a dream that all came to nothing? Why have me go through all that pain, training, sacrifice, and commitment, and have Joy deal with the struggles of me traveling so much, if it wasn't going to amount to anything?

And why would God lead me down a path where I was convinced I was going to win a gold medal and tell people about Him, only to see it turn to dust? Why? Why would He give me this dream to be like John Peterson and win gold and be an amazing man who inspired thousands upon thousands of people as he traveled the world? And why would He let me lose to Matt Lindland in such a bad way? It's one thing to lose, it's a whole other thing to lose the way I did; he owned me that day. He took a piece of me that I would never get back.

The questions went unanswered. So I asked them again. And when I'd asked every single one I could think of, and asked them all a hundred times more, I sat in the silence and allowed bitterness to flood in. I felt bitter for what Matt had done, bitter at the way I had not fought, bitter for the fact that God appeared to have stepped back and left me alone. The sense of negativity was immense, almost overwhelming. At times it felt as though I would never be able to breathe again. Since I had learned to flip the switch, I had hardly ever let another opponent own me. My last match had been the worst one I had ever fought and I had allowed him to control the fight and own me. I was going to have to find a way of living with the knowledge that my wrestling career did not finish strong.

Gradually, slowly, the pain eased. Back in Colorado Springs, I was alone in the house one day. The Olympics had been and gone. I hadn't watched much of them on the TV, but I'd seen enough. I'd watched Carl Lewis win another gold, saw Michael Jonson pick up two more. I'd watched as the reports of the bombing came in, and turned off when the coverage switched to the wrestling.

Gordy Morgan had won the USA team trials, and he ended up finishing 9th. The gold medalist was a Cuban guy I'd lost to on the one occasion we'd faced each other in Colombia, where the match took place with armed guards protecting the US team from angry crowds. I wondered how many points my home field advantage would have been worth had I met him in Atlanta.

But all that was behind me. There was no point in going over those old wounds. Better to stick to what I knew to be true: I had a wife I loved, two beautiful children, and a house that looked out on the tall trees standing guard on the flat ground before the mountains that kept Colorado Springs in place. There was a lot to be thankful for. But still the questions weighed heavy upon me. Still I had no idea what the rest of my life was going to hold. I was 28 and I was finished. What else was there to say?

I did a lot of talking out loud in those days. I would stand in the kitchen and look out at the trees. They called it Black Forest and the name was a perfect fit. At times the things I said sounded angry, at other times sad. Sometimes, I just sounded tired. "God," I prayed one evening, sighing with the familiarity of the words. "I wanted to go win a gold medal for you. I really did."

The strangest thing happened. It was as if a thought came into my head, but I hadn't placed it there. "I don't need you to do great things for me. I don't need you to win gold medals for me. I want to do great things in and through you."

I knew God's voice. So many times through the years I had felt as though I had heard Him, and this was the clearest one of all. Straight away the words resonated within me. I knew I had given my best and fallen short – my attempts to be great and impressive had failed. There must be something better ahead, I just knew it.

Before I could think about it anymore, the phone rang.

"Hello?"

"Dan Russell? This is John Peterson. I hope you don't mind me calling you at home..."

Chapter eleven

THE PRISON

I had so many images of John Peterson in my mind. There was the John Peterson I had watched on our very first TV set: hazy, colorful footage of him winning gold at the Montreal Olympics and me choosing him as the hero I was going to follow. There was the John Peterson who had looked down at me from the poster on my wall: strong-jawed, determined, always calling me on to dig deeper, push harder, and train better. Then there was the John Peterson I had met at a handful of matches over the years; I'd struggled for words every time, but the warmth of his smile and the strength of his handshake always left me feeling as though I was doing something right.

What were the chances of the man behind all these significant memories calling me at home at 10:30 on a winter's evening? I decided they were so implausibly slim that whoever was on the phone telling me his name was John Peterson was clearly not John Peterson. I cleared my throat, sighing as I replied. "Hey, Dad. What's up?"

"Sorry?" came the reply. "I was hoping to speak with Dan Russell. It's John Peterson speaking."

"Yeah, I know Dad. You've got the voice pretty good. You got me!"

"Oh, I see. This really is John Peterson. I'm not joking."

I'm still a little embarrassed even today by how long we went back and forth like this on the phone that evening. But, eventually, I came to the conclusion that it wasn't a prank call from my dad to cheer me up. It really was my childhood hero on the phone.

"How are you doing, Dan?" he said once I had finally stopped being suspicious and started being nervous.

"Fine," I replied. "You know, I'm OK. I think." The truth was I was feeling anything but fine or OK. The truth was I was feeling disillusioned and sad and, strangely, kind of lonely. The cause that had determined what I ate, when I woke up, what I forced my body to do and my mind to overcome, the very thing that had occupied more of my waking thoughts than any other element of my life, was now gone. I was grieving but there had never even been a funeral.

I was used to pain. All my life I had known what it was to hurt, not just in my body, but within my emotions too. And all my life I'd seen that if I pushed through the pain, eventually it passed. If I worked hard enough through the struggles, then good things would come as a result. But I had never felt pain like I had since losing to Matt Lindland. My body had started to revolt, as if it had stored up a list of complaints over two decades and was now presenting them to me as a reminder of what I had put it through. My soul was in worse shape though, and my greatest fear was that the pain of life as an ex-wrestler was the one challenge I was not going to be able to push myself through. I was going to say that I was fine again, but thought better of it. Instead John filled the silence.

"Dan, in September I'm going to the former Soviet Union with some guys. We're going to do a bunch of wrestling clinics and tell people about Jesus. I want you to come with me."

In the months that followed the call I went on something of a journey. As soon as John had asked me to join him on the trip I wanted to shout "yes" at him with all the force and volume I had used whenever I started a wrestling practice. But I was also unsure. I understood that God didn't need me to be impressive or great, but I couldn't help feeling that my final wrestling match had revealed some deep character flaws within me. It was my fault, not God's. Could I really stand up and be a leader when I felt so unsure about what the next phase of my life would contain?

Wrestling had taught me a lot. I wrestled with the challenge that I had let Matt own me. I had let him break me. John Peterson never let that happen to him. Did he really want me on the team? Besides, I was wrestling a bit with God on my own as well. Could I trust Him with whatever was going to come next? All my life

I had set goals and followed training plans, both the destination and my journey to get there clearly mapped out ahead of me. With wrestling now over, could I learn to let go and trust God for the next adventure?

I was not angry with God – I'd worked through enough of that in my college years – but I was angry with myself. Did I even believe that I deserved for God to do something great through me? That was the ultimate question. Could I forgive myself for what I had done?

Finally, sometime between speaking to John on the phone and boarding the plane to Moscow, I learned to answer "yes" to all those questions. Finally I learned that it was possible to trust God with my pain, to find Him present in it, to hear Him speaking gently to me in my pain.

On the plane with John and a couple of wrestlers I had trained beside before my last match, I sat awake and wondered what on earth God might do through me that could be considered great. Could it be that this trip might be the start of it? Maybe so. Maybe this was the opening of a new chapter of my life.

For two weeks we traveled around the former Soviet Union. Winter was coming and the temperatures fell as we witnessed what seemed to be a never-ending parade of tall, gray concrete apartment blocks, slept beneath quilts as thick as a mattress, and drank tea brewed in silver samovars.

From the minute we arrived I was like a little kid, desperate to be the first one to the car, the table, or the boarding gate so I could sit next to John and hear him talk. I didn't mind what he spoke about; I just liked hearing him and experiencing the fulfillment of a childhood dream that was coming true in a way I could never have imagined. Not only was I with my hero, but I started to believe God was up to something. For the first time in my adult life, I began to sense that my twin roles of pastor and wrestler need not be kept separate at all. Maybe there was a way of bringing them together?

"The thing about Christianity," John told me one day as we crossed a border into yet another country with identical concrete walls and heavy skies, "is that it is thought to be only for sick, old, naive women. Around here Christians are objects of scorn, they're to be pitied. But wrestlers, now they're another story altogether. They're the heroes, they're the model of strength and honor. They're the ones that people look up to. So we're in for some fun here, Dan. God has a plan for us."

It turned out he was right. We arrived late in the evening and were introduced to our hosts. Mine was Oleg, a guy about my size. It was clear he was a wrestler, and when I asked him what he did as we drove back to his apartment, he told me he was in business; "goot business," to be precise. I must have looked confused, so he carried on. "When people don't pay, I make them pay." Flashing me a smile and showing me a hefty gold watch he added, "Goot business, da?"

He told me before we got to his apartment he would have to attend to some of his business, which consisted of him pulling his Lada up outside a shop that sold vodka and little more, walking up to the counter and holding out his hand while the startled-looking owner handed over a thick wad of notes. He counted the money, put some of it in his pocket and gave the rest back. "Goot business," Oleg said as we drove off. "They give me money, I give them protection."

"What if they don't give you the money?" I asked.

"I break them."

Back home he pulled out a bottle of vodka and suggested that we both have a drink, "Leetle, leetle wodka, da?" I told him I didn't drink and listened as he told me again and again that he didn't have a drinking problem. Ten shots later, with his head down the toilet, I wondered whether he still believed his own story. But I liked Oleg. I liked him a lot.

We had arranged part of the trip with the help of some local missionaries – men and women who took great risks to share their faith in this culturally Muslim country, and as we prepared for our first event, their leader came to find us. "What you're doing here has never happened before," he said, his voice quiet against the sound of chairs being laid out and tables cleared. "But you need to be careful. Some of the men you've invited here tonight are dangerous people. If they found out we are Christian missionaries there could be real trouble for us. The people gathering tonight are the very people we are careful to not reveal our identity to. You have the top political, business, and sports people in the community, all very powerful, influential people and none of them like Christians at all. This is extremely dangerous!"

I could see his point, but my faith in John and the rest of the team – as well as the power of wrestling in that culture – was strong. We prayed, sensing this was all part of the reason for the trip and that God had a plan. We went ahead with the banquet and watched as the people we had invited filed in to the room. Wearing their thick winter coats and stern expressions, they looked every inch like the collection of mafia, corrupt politicians, and petty crooks the missionary had warned us about. And yet they had taken up our invitation which we had sent throughout the wrestling community to join us for an evening banquet with a talk from an American Olympic gold medalist.

It felt so much like the feast that had closed the Poddubny tournament, yet different too. I was an observer, not part of the focus, but it bothered me less than I thought it might. After the plates had been cleared away, John stood up to speak. I had never heard him preach before; the only public speaking I had seen him do was at wrestling tournaments where he would stand above us all and talk about what it took to be a champion.

Here in the room full of formidable men with cauliflower ears, the air heavy with the smell of cheap cologne and even cheaper tobacco, John began by talking about the Koran. He was gentle, kind, sometimes funny but never irreverent. He talked about what the Koran said about Jesus, and with every word he spoke, the men seemed to listen harder and harder. When he had finished talking about their holy book, he paused. "And now I want to tell you what Jesus says about himself. The Koran speaks of Jesus as a great prophet, but he was more than a prophet. I want to tell you what the Bible says about Jesus."

Still the audience leaned in, still hanging on John's words as if the banquet had awoken some deeper hunger within them that John's words were now satisfying. He talked about the man described in the Bible as God's only son, how he wrestled with Satan, how he wrestled with fear, how he grabbed hold of death and won. He talked about his courage in the face of people who wanted him dead and his compassion for those cast out by society. The room was silent except for John's words, motionless except for his gentle moving about to and fro as he spoke from the floor. As he drew to a close he ended by holding up a video that had been dubbed into Russian and told the story of Jesus. "We have a copy for you if anyone here would like one. Just come up and see us and we will be happy to give you one."

People didn't just walk forward, they ran. We gave out over two hundred videos that night as people crushed forward, fearful that we were going to run out.

The next night, back at Oleg's apartment, there was a crowd of people as his family gathered to say good-bye before I left the next day. One proposed a toast and placed a shot glass in my hand, but I reminded Oleg that I didn't drink. He shrugged and translated the message back to people, but it only made things worse. Everyone started talking angrily at once. "Oleg, what did you say?" I asked.

"I told them you don't drink because you are Christian." I remembered the warning that the missionary had given us and wondered if I should have been more careful, but Oleg stood up and quieted them down.

I listened as he spoke for five minutes, watching the faces in the room turn from anger and confusion to something else. When he had finished speaking and a handful of individual conversations had started up, quietly, throughout the room, I asked what he had said.

"I tell them about what John Peterson said. I tell them about Jesus." He paused and smiled. "And now I have just one more leetle, leetle wodka, da?" Then we all sat down to watch the Jesus film we had given out the night before.

The next day we left Oleg and the community of crooks and wrestlers with their videos and moved on. Our next visit was to an orphanage and we arrived with a TV, a VCR, and a tape of The Miracles of Jesus in cartoon form that had been dubbed into Russian. We thought it would be a brilliant way to capture their imagination and teach them about God, but as the cartoon played, the room full of three-, four-, and five-year-olds began to unravel. Within minutes they were wrestling among themselves, running up and down the tattered room in front of the TV. I went to the front to turn it off, but was stopped by one of the missionaries we were with. "No. Watch," he said.

So we carried on watching as the room continued to get louder and louder, the bodies running faster and faster and the little cartoon drifted further and further from the center of attention. It was painful to watch, but in time it was over and the missionary called the kids to come back and sit down. Translating for us as he went, he asked, "So what were the miracles that Jesus did?"

Every hand went up. Not one single miracle was missed.

The rest of the day was just as powerful. I saw how the children lived, how they were cared for and loved by good people, but how still they had a natural longing to be with families of their own. I handed out little buttons someone had given me before I left; simple things with "You are 1 in 5.7 billion" printed on them. I hadn't really known why I had packed them, but as I passed them around to each of the children and watched them display them with the same pride as an Olympic medalist, I was glad I did.

John was buried under a mountain of moving parts as some of the children spent much of the afternoon climbing all over him. There were two on his arms, one on his back, a little guy hanging from his neck, and an even smaller guy sitting in his lap, talking non-stop into John's face. Whenever John looked away the tiny kid reached up and grabbed his face, making sure he had John's full attention.

"What's going on?" I asked.

"I don't know," he smiled. "Maybe this little guy needs to go to the bathroom. He's been on me a while. Is that what he's saying?"

"No," replied the missionary. "He's asking if you will be his daddy."

The tears came slowly at first, but soon John was flooded, weeping over this tiny child. I cried too, but not so much for the kid. It was John that moved me; the sight of one of the toughest men ever to have walked the planet, sitting on a bare floor with children climbing all over him while he hunched over the smallest of the bunch, his shoulders heaving up and down. I'd always admired him for his medals and his wrestling glory, but in that moment I saw the real truth about what inspired me about John Peterson. He was strong and he was brave, but he was something else as well... not vulnerable, but something better than that. He was woundable. He was exactly the kind of man that I wanted to be, exactly the kind of man I had thought so much about in those days of childhood dreams fueled by my dad. Being there without my brother made me miss Joe even more.

I had so many conversations with John about what it meant to be a champion, and gradually things were starting to make sense. Maybe my lack of a gold medal – or anything at all from the Olympics – wasn't the failure I thought it was. Maybe the real measure of a champion was something that score sheets and trophy cabinets could never fully quantify.

We saw plenty of poverty on the trip, and experienced so much warmth and affection from our various hosts that it was soon impossible to look at those concrete apartment blocks and bare-earth sidewalks in the same way. But as we pulled up outside the venue for one of our final parts of the tour, I couldn't help but feel intimidated.

We had arrived at a prison, miles from the nearest town. It was colder out here than any of the other places we had been, and the wind tore across the flat landscape at will. Besides the twin layers of twelve foot high razor wire fence and the squat gray building behind it, there was nothing else to see. We waited in the van outside the main gate while a guard ambled over to check our papers. We told him we had been invited by the prison director, who had heard about our wrestling demonstration. He didn't smile at all, but we were used to that by now. Once he was satisfied, he invited us to leave the car and join him at the gate for a safety briefing, which he delivered while rolling a cigarette with one hand.

"He says this is a maximum security prison," said Stephen Barrett, our translator. Stephen had been a wrestler himself but had been working underground preaching and traveling throughout the former USSR for years. He knew how to get around officials and he knew when to back off. Though I felt like I was out of my depth already, Stephen's tone of voice was light and relaxed. "He says it's full of the worst criminals in the country. He says that half of the inmates have tuberculosis and nearly all of them have lice. And when we walk through the gate don't step off the path, otherwise we'll get blown up by a land mine."

With that, the guard waved us through. I looked carefully at the flat earth around us as we passed the gate, but I couldn't see any land mines, and that bothered me. Inside the building smelled of rust and cold and sickness. We were ushered into a warm office furnished

with a heavy wooden desk at the center and small
chairs backed up against the walls all around.

The prison director was polite and friendly and
talked about how he had put on a special dinner for us.
He had invited lots of important people and hoped we
would all be comfortable. John reminded him that we
had only agreed to come if we could meet some prisoners and put on a wrestling display for them.

"Yes," said the director. "I know. But I must tell you
that you are only second visitors ever to this prison.
Last group was guards from Cuba who want to see how
to set up good prison like ours. That was thirteen years
ago. Nobody ever want to see prisoners."

"We know," said John. "But if we can't see them,
we're going to have to miss the banquet."

The director puffed out his fat cheeks. "Is ok," he
said. "But remember these are bad men. They are
dangerous and they are dirty. You do not touch any of
them, understand?"

We agreed. The thought of touching anyone didn't
appeal to me at all. I would have no problem sticking to
the rules. The director spoke briefly into a phone and
told us that the men would soon be ready for us.

We left his office a few minutes later and were taken
to what must have been the dining area, though I could
see no tables or even enough chairs for half the crowd
of men gathered there. On the way we had passed

some cells, each one filled with rows of bunk beds. It reminded me of the Holocaust films I had seen over the years. Everywhere the smell of bodily fluids was oppressive. It was as if no fresh air ever made it this far into the prison, and even the feeble lights struggled against the fumes.

But it was the men that really shocked me. They were all thin, all with shaven heads, all wearing the same grey tattered uniforms. For a moment I thought I had stumbled across a relic of World War II, and I half expected to see yellow Stars of David sewn onto their frail-looking chests. All of them sat or stood in the same way: their hands clasped together in front of their chests as if holding something close to their hearts for fear of losing it. Those that did look up from the floor displayed Holocaust eyes that were pale and weak, lacking almost any sign of life at all.

All of us wrestlers were silenced by what we saw, and as we stood and stared I remembered the words of Albert Camus: "To lose one's life is no great matter; when the time comes I'll have the courage to lose mine. But what's intolerable is to see one's life being drained of meaning, to be told there's no reason for existing. A man can't live without some reason for living."

As far as I could tell, these men had no reason for living. They were a people without any purpose, their bodies merely existing while their souls had clearly long since given up the fight. Armed guards stood around the edge of the room, their weapons at the ready, but I doubted whether there was any one of them who had the strength or the life left in him to present any kind of threat.

We rolled out the camel hair rugs we had been using as wrestling mats and went through our demonstration. The two grapplers on our team turned up the heat as they threw and tumbled together like strong men of old. Any other crowd would have played along, applauding the strength and stamina of the men on display; but not these guys. There were a thousand or so inmates that watched us as the evening began, and all of their faces remained blank. No response. They just sat there with empty gazes on their faces. Our display made no impact at all. The guys finished up their wrestling and Stephen stepped out in front of the mats.

He spoke in Russian to the men, and as soon as he had finished his first sentence it was clear he had caused a stir. "What did you say?" we asked, against the background noise that had suddenly risen up. "I asked if there is anybody here who wants to wrestle one of us."

Much of the noise in the room was coming from the corner of the room, and from there a lone figure got to his feet. The room erupted with chants of "Sergei! Sergei!" and the guards edged forward nervously. In an instant the men had been transformed from breathing corpses to rowdy wrestling fans as they cheered their hero toward the front.

Sergei had the ears of a wrestler, but not the physique. His clothes hung from him and his face was old and drawn. Stephen said something to him in Russian and I watched as Sergei scanned the line of us wrestlers. Slowly he lifted his hand and stuck a finger out in my direction.

"Yego," he said.

Stephen turned to me. "He said he wants to fight you, Dan." I looked at Sergei, who I was convinced definitely had TB, and then at the guards. They were holding their guns higher now, shouting at the men nearest them to sit down. Seeing the look of panic on my face, Stephen added, "This is what we are here for. Let's do it, Dan. Let's go!"

I stood on the mat opposite my opponent. He could well have been big one day, but it was hard to tell now. I wondered what I should do; could I really wrestle him? I'd break something if I even used a quarter of my strength on a gut wrench. I could have probably blown on him and he'd have fallen over.

He started coming at me, shoulders down, arms in, head moving unsteadily from side to side, his eyes locked onto mine. I grabbed him by his shoulders, pushing his arms in to his sides and gently took him to the ground. It was no fight, but Sergei and I never broke eye contact throughout. Somehow we made a connection.

"I'm going to ask if anyone else wants to come up," said Stephen, and as soon as he spoke in Russian the guards and director rushed up as if to stop it. Somehow they stepped back, though I don't know why. Perhaps they saw something in Stephen's face that made them think twice. Whatever the reason, what happened next was pure chaos. The room had been absolutely still and lifeless until we offered this wrestling challenge. At last we were speaking a language that these men understood. With the whole room cheering another five or six wrestlers came up to the mat, each of them squaring up to one of us before being laid gently down on the mat. We stacked them up like prey at a game reserve, only they were no trophies and they were far from dead. As they lay there, grinning up at us, they looked more alive than anyone I had ever seen.

"Dan," Stephen was touching my arm. "Would you now preach to them?"

I was shocked. So far on the trip I hadn't preached once, and that was fine with me. I'd spoken about wrestling a bit, mentioning what it was like to win the Poddubny and how I had always admired the Russian way of wrestling, but I had never spoken anything about God.

"I don't have anything planned," I said back to Stephen.

"Nobody does," he replied. "God has a plan. He loves these men. And He wants them to know it. The world may have forgotten them but God has not, and we are here to let them know that. You'll be fine."

I took a breath and tried to remember the calm

feeling I used to have before I started a match. I could wait no longer, so I said the first thing that came into my head. "If you throw a little pebble into a pond you get a little splash, a little ripple, and then the pebble will sink to the bottom. If you take a big rock and throw it into the pond and you'll get a big splash and big ripples but the rock too will end up at the bottom. Sin is sin. Sin drags all of us to the bottom. Some of us just make a bigger splash than others. I'm no different from you."

I went on to tell them about Jesus and talk about what He came to do. I talked about how He sacrificed Himself so that none would be lost. I told them that everyone could be found, everyone could be rescued, even prisoners here in the middle of nowhere.

People started to cheer and clap, but one man's voice shouted out louder than all the others. "Hallelujah! Hallelujah!" said a man at the back, so loud that it felt as though the whole prison was reverberating with the sound of his voice.

One by one the men all came up to the front, but not to wrestle this time. Instead they wanted to shake our hands. One man that made his way forward was the man who had shouted "hallelujah" and as he paused to speak, he told us his story which Stephen translated.

"He says he has been praying a lot lately. He's the only Christian in the prison and he was thrown in here because he was a pastor. He says he's been asking God to send someone to encourage him, and then we show up! He says he's overwhelmed by how much God loves him that he would send us here. And he has one more request to God. He wants to have a Bible."

I was amazed at this last bit. If it had been me I would have been pleading with the visitors to get me out, but this guy just wanted a Bible so he could learn more about God while he was in prison. As he shared his story, I was reminded of the shallowness of my faith when I had faced difficult situations. I had been struggling with not making the Olympic team, but this guy was struggling to survive in a prison that was a living graveyard.

Eventually, after every single one of them had shaken each of our hands, the prison director approached. He was smiling. "You have to come back," he said. "We've never seen anything like this."

With the story of the pastor prisoner still ringing in our ears, Stephen spoke up. "Well," he said with a gentle firm authority that was more of a statement than a question. "We don't have much time left. But we have some friends that live nearby and they will come back next week if that is OK? And they are going to bring in some Bibles for every prisoner here."

A few days later, that's exactly what happened. Some underground missionary friends went back to the prison, handing a Bible to every prisoner there.

For days after that first visit to the prison, I couldn't stop thinking about what this pastor had told me.

Somehow, in the few words it took for him to tell his story, I heard enough to complete a change within me that had been edging slowly forward for months.

There are times in life when you look back and realize how petty you are. As I cried in the prison I remembered all the times I'd complained at God for not letting me win a gold medal. But right there in front of me was a pastor who didn't just lose a chance for glory; he lost his entire freedom just so he could be used by God. The only way to reach those other men in the prison was for one of them to be so loyal and faithful to God that he would keep on praying, keep on believing even when he was locked up, shaved, malnourished, diseased, and neglected. That was the kind of faith I wanted to have, not the sort that threw a tantrum just because I missed out on Olympic glory.

I had felt so guilty for not finishing strong, guilty for letting myself, my family, and God down when it mattered most. But I didn't want that to be the end of my story. All throughout the trip I had been amazed by what I had seen, how I was experiencing things that I'd dreamed of my whole life; being a wrestler among wrestlers but talking about God. And yet it hadn't taken a gold medal to do it; not any gold medal of mine, at least.

Now the window was being thrown even wider; could I allow God to use me just as He wanted to?

Of all the goals I had ever set, that was the one I wanted to achieve the most.

On the very last morning of the trip we spent an hour or so with some young wrestlers in their club. So many of the boys there had no proper wrestling shoes, and instead wrestled in beat up tennis shoes and socks. After the workout, one boy started to talk to me in broken English. "I like your shoes, meester."

"Oh, these Nikes? They're the best." I was going to tell him what made them so great and how it was cool to be sponsored by Nike and get free stuff all the time, but I thought better of it. Instead I undid my laces and held them out to him. "Take them, please."

"I cannot. I have nothing to give you in return."

"I don't mind," I said. "They're a gift. You don't have to give me anything in return."

He looked troubled. "Let me go home now and bring you gift."

"Nope! We're leaving now. You're just going to have to keep them, and if you really want to give a gift in return, give it to one of your teammates, OK?"

He shrugged, smiled, and took the shoes. I never did get to leave my shoes on the mat the way you're supposed to when you retire. Somehow this felt like a far better way to mark the change in my wrestling journey. I was no longer going to compete, but I was far from finished. God had plans for me, I was sure.

Chapter twelve

COACH

Throughout my life I had been influenced by the great coaches I had trained under. My dad had instilled the dream. Coach Sprague focused on the minute details of each aspect of every technique, all the time expecting excellence. Coach Katsen brought out the tiger in me. Coach Miyake opened my eyes to the value of each person on the team. Coach Houck taught me the will to win. Coach Grahn gave me a deeper love for the sport. Coach Fraser introduced the Grind Match and Coach Petrosyan showed me the journey to the top of the world.

Each of these coaches has influenced me, yet of all of them it is my father who has shaped me the most. I always knew he loved Joe and me more than life itself, and I am so glad I was able to embrace the strong work ethic that he demonstrated.

Dan and Coach Masao Miyake

And I knew that, as a Christian, it was God who was his

boss. Just as I was answerable to him, so he was answerable to God.

Like a good father, a good coach pushes you beyond what you think you are capable of doing. Even though your body screams for rest, a good coach will call out of you the knowledge that they know best and can be trusted. A good coach calls out the champion, no matter how well hidden it may be.

There was more to all of my coaches than the wrestling. Each of them had opened my eyes to a fundamental truth in life. They had each taught me lessons that didn't expire when I retired. The older I got, the more I came to value and rely on their legacy.

Together, my coaches had helped me to reach a place where I could imagine a world that was bigger than the sport. Thanks to them I was able to begin to see how wrestling was just a tool in God's hand; how it could be used to shape me into the man He had created me to be. And while I approached coaching with a firm desire to call out of other young men the champion in life as well as the on the mat, I found that God had more lessons for me to learn as well.

The next time I went to Russia, there were no tear-stained trips to orphanages or fear-fueled visits to maximum security prisons. But there was a growing sense that I was in the right place, doing the right thing.

I was with the US team as they returned to the Poddubny tournament, held again in the gray snow and austere architecture of Perm. It was good to be back and shake the hands of many people who remembered me from the previous year, but I was more focused on the matches ahead than the thrill of the past. We had a great team with us and were looking for success, especially from the big guy I had been working with for weeks. Rulon Gardner was unknown on the scene but we all knew he had the potential to make it. And Poddubny '97 was going to be his breakout year.

It was all going so well until we hit a wall – a six foot, three and a quarter inch wall of muscle and pain. He was called Alexander Karelin and he was the single greatest fighter of his generation. Even as a baby he was impressive, weighing in at fifteen pounds, and he had been undefeated since 1987. Alexander the Great, The Siberian Bear, The Experiment – whatever you called him, the truth was undeniable; he was a giant made of steel and muscle, and he was one of the toughest wrestlers of all time.

I don't know how we thought Rulon was going to win against him, but we thought he had a shot. But as I watched from the corner of the mat I saw Karelin take my guy apart. It was ugly. Karelin showed his power and expertise and the final result wasn't even close, though the five to zero score doesn't tell the full story: how Rulon was thrown on his face three times, how Karelin had flipped the 290 pounder like a toddler in a playground. Rulon and the rest of us left Russia knowing there were just three short years to figure out how to beat this legendary champ.

Rulon and I had wrestled together, roomed together, traveled together, and trained together. Though my wrestling days were done, I had the privilege of seeing my friend dedicate himself to the task as the Sydney Olympics in 2000 approached. Rulon worked hard, fought a lot of matches, and believed he could deliver one of the biggest upsets in the history of wrestling.

And that's exactly what he did. Rulon and Karelin made it to the Olympic final and there were barely a handful of people in the room who believed that Rulon had a hope. Karelin had stated before that it would be his final match, and various officials from the Olympic Committee had gathered in the venue to crown the inevitable winner and celebrate a thirteen year winning streak.

But Rulon fought for every hold. He stayed present. He embraced the battle. Having not lost a single point in ten years, Karelin went down one to nothing in the second round. The crowd and officials were shocked, and I'm convinced that the fear started to mess with Karelin's head. Though Karelin tried to throw Rulon, he simply couldn't manage it. Rulon refused to be beaten.

I watched the match on TV, aware that I was witnessing history being made. And as I saw my friend celebrate with a cartwheel on the mat, I knew there couldn't be many better illustrations of the importance of not trying to win the medal or even trying to win the match. All we ever need to do is fight to win the moment. Focus on that, and the winning will take care of itself.

As I spent more time coaching, I noticed that I was learning other truths as well. I traveled to Egypt with the World Junior Team in 1998 against the backdrop of growing tension between the US and Iraq. President Clinton had launched Operation Desert Fox not long before, and the flyby bombings did not make the US popular in the Middle East.

The tournament organizers had a little fun at our expense, seating me opposite the Iraqi coach at a pre-tournament meeting, but after the matches began, we became aware that we were at risk of something worse than a little social awkwardness. We had some private US security traveling with us, led by an ex-secret service guy named Larry Buendorf.

Larry had served three US presidents and thwarted one assassination attempt. He was capable and professional, and everywhere we went, he made sure we were given explicit instructions in the case of emergency. We were told from which door we were to exit in an emergency and to go to bed every night in our military hotel with all our gear packed. I felt responsible for my team members and each night I would go room to room to check on them. One night, when tensions had been running higher than usual, I found every room was empty. I was starting to get a little concerned as I came to the last room and found them all huddled together. They were nervous and thought that if someone tried to do something and saw the empty rooms, they might think we were no longer there.

One night, just after 1 a.m., the phone in my room

rang. "Mr. Russell? This is reception. Get your team up and downstairs immediately." We'd listened well to Larry and had our bags packed the night before, so we were down in reception within a few minutes.

"Get in the bus," said the hotel security guard. I didn't know what was going on, but I guessed it was some security threat and we needed to move quickly. But just as we were about to board, one of our team called out, "Coach, where's our security? Where's Larry?" He was right. All through the trip we had had Larry or his team at our side – apart from at night when they slept in a different hotel. But if we were going to be taken some-where by a driver we'd never seen on a bus we'd never sat in, shouldn't we at least have our security with us?

We walked back to reception and I told the desk clerk that we weren't going anywhere without our security. The guy started shouting at me, "You need to get on the bus. No time to waste." The angrier he got, the easier it was to stick to our line and refuse to move. All night we sat in the lobby, waiting for Larry and his team to arrive, but they never did. Eventually, when the recep-tion night staff left and the new people arrived, all talk of us getting on the bus – as well as the bus itself – simply vanished.

It made me think a lot about fear and how easy it us for us to make wrong choices when the adrenaline is surging. Throughout life there are people trying to urge us onto the bus – to try this experience, to compromise that principle, to cross these lines and abandon those ideals – and so much of the time they use fear to hurry us ahead. In life, as in wrestling, fear always leads to bad decisions.

Toward the end of that Egypt trip, we watched in the tournament room as an Israeli wrestler won his weight division. As was customary, when the athlete climbed up to the top of the podium, my teammates and I got to our feet. Apart from the Germans and handful of Israelis, we were the only nation that did so. Everybody else was seated, even the stand full of soldiers in full uniform, bearing enough small arms to start a war. And while the national anthem played, the room erupted into a symphony of whistles and shouts, stamps and yells that all but drowned out the official anthem of Israel. Some people hurled objects into the center of the arena, but like the few dozen others, I stood there, refusing to give in to fear.

I knew that by standing I was a target, but I wanted to show honor where honor was due. I wanted to stand for this wrestler in the same way that I wanted to stand for God. I wanted to stand for finishing strong, not hide away. Besides, I was beginning to know for myself that God had a plan for me and my life. He alone numbers our days. He alone can give us true purpose.

I felt the same way some years later when I was in Iran. In many ways the country is the home of wrestling, and just like the trip to Egypt there was a palpable sense of tension. I stayed with host families and saw first-hand their love of wrestling. A crowd of 15,000 gathered in the stadium to watch the tournament, with an estimated 10,000 standing outside, the noise of their chanting forcing its way into the arena. The anti-American feeling was high, and as I sat in the coaches' corner I could feel my back and head being pelted with things – mostly just pocket change. But I didn't blame them; they just wanted to demonstrate their passion. Even though those coins can cause quite a sting, I pretended not to feel a thing. I kept my eyes focused on the match ahead. Nothing else mattered.

In spite of the reception we received when we were on the mat, I have never experienced a culture that was more gracious as hosts. Their national training facility was the most impressive I have ever set my foot in and as I had the opportunity to enter their world, my view of them changed. I moved from feeling the need to pretend their passion meant nothing to me, to wanting to encourage and bless them in any way I could. So when I got the opportunity to go on state TV and talk about wrestling, I politely asked while on air if I could pray a blessing on their nation, thanking God for them. They said yes, and I had the privilege of praying for them live on TV.

The last match of that trip was one I will never forget. Our heavyweight, Brian Keck, came out and wrestled for the bronze. He was fired up and he took to the mat like a bull. By this point we had won the crowd over and they liked our intensity and our love for the sport. Brian was as intense as anyone else and ran his opponent right off the mat, all the way to the center of the other mat. The crowd erupted, but this time with pleasure.

I had coached Brian for several years, but I knew nothing about his personal story. As we traveled home I asked him how he got here. What he told me left me stunned.

Brian was given up for adoption at the age of two. His parents thought he was mentally handicapped and came to the conclusion that raising a child with this disability would be too difficult for them. So they sent him to an orphanage. But just one year later, doctors found out that Brian wasn't in any way mentally handicapped; he was just deaf in one ear.

After corrective surgery on his ear, Brian was able to hear perfectly. At four, a family adopted him, feeling sorry for him because of what his parents had done. Their pity did not grow into love. Over the next several years they told Brian on a regular basis that they were sorry they ever adopted him. They told him they did not love him. He was verbally and physically abused. One day, when he was eleven, Brian was called to the principal's office at school. The principal told him he would not be going home to his adoptive family ever again. His dad had called the police that morning and told them if Brian came home, he was going to kill him. His dad continued by saying that he would kill his wife, and then he would take his own life.

Brian was immediately placed into foster care. He lived in 28 different homes, four adoptive-to-be homes, and two group homes over the next five years. He bounced from school to school and was given no chance to succeed.

I listened as he told me all this, shocked at the enormity of all he had endured. If anyone should have been bitter, it was Brian. He could have drowned himself in toxic tears and everyone would have understood. Nothing that had happened to him was Brian's fault. He was a victim.

But he wasn't. Brian refused to see himself this way. He graduated from high school and earned a college scholarship as a state high school wrestling champion. He went on to graduate from junior college as the national junior college champion, and from there to a university where he graduated with a degree in social work. Driving all this was a desire to help kids that were going through the same things he experienced as a child.

I'd known Brian for years but never had a clue about his difficult past. And I probably would never have known about it had I not asked him. As he finished telling me his story, he added two more comments that have never left me. "Dan," he said, "I had a terrible past, that is true, but I would not change a thing about it. My past made me who I am today, and I like me."

I was just absorbing this when he carried on talking. "It's true, horrible things happened to me, but why would I dwell on the past when I have such a great future?"

As much as my coaches shaped my character, my experiences as a coach continued to exert an influence upon me. As I watched others struggle, I saw a reflection of my own weaknesses. As I saw wrestlers embrace the fight, I was reminded of the hard work I needed to apply to my own life. And though I was becoming aware of how I still had a long way to go to match up to the champ that I believed God was building me up to be, I knew that it was possible.

God's plans are bigger than we think, dream, or imagine. Whether we are hoping to be an elite sportsperson or a great parent, a leader in business or a loyal friend and person of integrity and honor, we all need to learn how to be coachable. That means listening to the hard truths and difficult assessments. It means doing the work the coach sets out before us with our whole heart. Like Coach Sprague reminded us every day, "the making of a champion is an intense burning desire." If we really do want to finish strong, we must learn to deal with our failures, to overcome our fears, and most importantly of all, to listen to the coach. It was a lesson my father had learned and that had also been passed on to Joe and me. As I became a coach myself, I too began to share the wisdom with the next generation.

Chapter thirteen

THE OLYMPICS

On a perfect eighty degree afternoon in late 2001, I stepped out of the six-seater plane and took in the view. It was exactly as I pictured it would be: lush trees offering bananas, mangoes, and passion fruit covered the hills on the mainland behind; a clear sky stretched the length of the ocean which flowed uninterrupted as far as I could see; children running across the grass toward the runway, calling out in anticipation of the treats they hoped to negotiate out of my fellow passengers. This was my first time visiting the island of Kosrae, but I could already feel myself giving in to its charms.

It wasn't just the fact that this tiny island north of Papua New Guinea looked, sounded, and felt like paradise. The Pacific Islands were working their way into my heart for other, nobler reasons. It all started some time after I had returned from the trip around the former Soviet Union with John Peterson. I had started working as an assistant coach at the USOTC, though I was unsure as to what I would do for the rest of my life. So when I heard the International Olympic Committee was looking for someone to come out to places like Pulau and the Federated States of Micronesia to see if they could teach people how to wrestle, it made as much sense as any other job I had considered.

At the time I didn't know what a big deal it was to get the job. Working on behalf of the International Olympic Solidarity program opened doors wherever I went, and the fact that I was there to nurture sport in a country that would otherwise struggle to find the resources to develop their own programs left me feeling like a cross between Willy Wonka and Muhammad Ali. "The Olympics are for everyone," I said whenever I was traveling as part of my new role, always surrounded by nodding officials and wide-eyed children. "Not just the wealthiest countries."

Dan is welcomed to Kosrae as Olympic Solidarity coach for the Federated States of Micronesia.

Because the Islanders are strong, agile, yet smaller than your typical person from the developed world, wrestling – with its weight classes – was a perfect sport for them to try. And it wasn't as if it was all new to them, either. Like pretty much every other culture on the planet, the Pacific Islanders have been wrestling in some way or another for generations. Or so I thought.

I was taken from the airstrip on Kosrae to a village where I was told to wait for the chief. I looked around and took it all in: simple timber buildings that looked as though they had been there for generations, people constantly chewing the betel nut that turned their teeth black. A small crowd had formed around me, mainly the usual throng of kids laughing at the sight of my pale, soft feet that poked out of my sandals. The crowd stirred and I looked up to see a skinny man striding toward me. He was a foot shorter than me, probably twenty or thirty years older, and with fewer teeth than I had fingers. After I was introduced, I gave my speech about what an honor it was to be here, how grateful I was that he had allowed me to visit, and how big and healthy the cow looked. As I spoke, he kept eyeing me up and down.

"We shall now wrestle," he said, motioning me forward with his hands. "We allow kicking, biting, scratching, and hair pulling," he explained, as someone took my bag from me and pushed me toward the chief. "But we allow no spitting." The next moment he crouched down and charged at me.

This was a challenge. I didn't fear the damage it might inflict on me as much as I feared what would happen after the match. If I won, he'd be shamed and I'd lose any chance of working with his village. If I lost, I'd be shamed and have nothing to offer. So I snapped his neck down and held him in a front headlock while we both shuffled around on the bare earth for a while.

After a while I could tell he'd had enough and that it was time to let go. "It is a draw!" he boomed, slapping me on the back.

Kosrae had a history, though like so much of history it's a little hard to separate out the fact from the myth. Someone once told me that for years everybody said Kosrae was the most wicked of all the islands. Missionaries came and left without making even one convert and the whole island was given over to fighting and drinking. Then some time before WWII the king had a dream one night. Nobody knows what he saw, but the next day he called the whole island together and said, "There is only room for one king on this island, and that king is Jesus." From that day on he removed his crown, abolished all titles on the island, and declared that everyone would now be equal under God. After the First World War, the Japanese came and brought with them new crops that the people had never heard of before. Soon the island was rich and happy in ways it had never been.

I've never found out whether that story about Kosrae's past is true, but so many people I spoke to agreed that the island's future was uncertain. With television about to arrive and the very first paved road due to be built, people were worried that the islanders might forget who they were altogether.

Even though I was there to teach them how to wrestle in line with the Olympic code, I knew that what I was doing was of great value. Of all the difficult things wrestling had given me – injuries, struggles, disappointment – it had given me so much more that had helped. It taught me courage, determination, and patience, things which the people of Kosrae would need in abundance when the modern world started to make its way onto the island.

For four years I helped oversee the development of the Olympic movement in the Federated States of Micronesia. Some of their wrestlers had real talent, and a few of them left the islands for a time and traveled to live with my family in the States. For the guy who came from an island with a population of just two hundred and had to travel by boat for two days just to reach the island of Yap, arriving at Portland International Airport was quite the thing.

I grew to love the culture of the islands and wherever I went, with every boat trip and island flight and sporting event with dozens of villagers standing and singing their ancient songs, I felt myself being drawn back to the love of sport that I knew as a child. The things my dad had done with me as a child – the way of inspiring others to greatness through the sport of wrestling – I was now getting to do with others.

I traveled a lot in those four years, always starting with a flight to Honolulu, then on to Guam and on to the islands. Guam became like a home away from home, and I got to know some of the local wrestlers out there. When one of their team was invited to take part in the 2004 Olympics in Athens under the Solidarity Program and I was invited to go along in support, I didn't hesitate to say yes. To be a part of the Games held in the original birthplace of the Olympics was a once in a lifetime opportunity that I was not going to miss.

We were a small group, just me and the wrestler, a couple of runners, a swimmer, their coaches, and the president of Guam's Olympic Committee. What we lacked in numbers we made up for in enthusiasm. We were one of the first teams to check into the village and I was desperate to get out and watch as much of the Games as I could.

The first event was the women's marathon. The stadium was packed with British fans, all there to see Paula Radcliffe do what everyone believed she would do and claim gold. We all knew the battle was for silver and bronze, and every time the jumbotron cut to Paula as she led the pack, the crowd went wild. Yet somewhere around mile sixteen she started to fall back, clearly struggling with the uphill course and hundred degree heat. Then, at mile twenty-three, the stadium fell silent as the screen was filled with the image of the greatest female marathon runner of her generation slowing, then stopping. She walked to the curb, sat with her head slung low and shoulders hunched.

I could never have predicted that the tears would come so forcefully. Yet I was a wreck, a sobbing, heaving wreck. I was crying uncontrollably, struggling for air as the images of Paula Radcliffe's failure filled my mind. She had come so close, had dedicated so much of her life, and yet had fallen short. I was weeping because of what had happened to her, but I knew I was really grieving my own loss.

My sobbing was loud and noisy, but soon it ceased and I could breathe again. I needed to grieve the loss of my wrestling career, but I did not need to be defined by it. It was not hard for me to see that this strange old journey I was on was in many ways so much better than the fantasy I had dreamed up as a child.

The next day the papers carried the story of the marathon, many of them leading with a quote from Paula Radcliffe where she explained why she stopped: "I could have finished but I realized with a few miles to go that I wouldn't win. And if I wasn't going to win, why run?"

My whole time in Athens was like a real time illustration of what I'd learned from a lifetime of sport. It almost appeared as though every interaction was designed to underline some point that I knew to be true from my own experience.

I worked with one of our runners, and tried hard to convey what a great privilege and rich experience it was to be able to compete here in Greece, the birthplace of the Olympics. I took her to the stadium a week before the heats for her distance, and tried to help her picture what it would be like to share this one moment with eighty thousand people. "When your name gets called and the camera pans to you, everyone here will be looking. There will be another two billion people around the world watching it on TV. You've got one shot at this, and it's the chance to show all of those people that you can run the very best race of your life. We're not here to win medals or even the heat, but to run for the honor of a personal best."

The speech sounded pretty good to me, but I knew it had missed the mark when a little later she said, "Coach, it would be great if we didn't have to run every day. This running's hard work."

On the day of the race, we got into the stadium and it was just as we imagined it would be. She looked so excited when her face filled the jumbotron, and the silence that settled in the seconds before the start of the race was magical. The gun fired, the runners set off, and I watched as my girl followed on. In a flash it was over. My runner was last, way at the back, but smiling and waving. "Coach! Coach! Coach!" she yelled as she came around to greet the Guam team. "I'm not even tired!"

In the nights that followed I heard her crying in her room. Maybe she realized she'd blown her opportunity; that she'd gone for a jog in the Olympic Games. Maybe she was grieving the end of her running career.

I wished I could have called out of her the greatness that I saw within her. I wished I could have coached her better, that somehow I could have inspired in her a hunger for doing her best at all times. But I hadn't managed either of those things.

Dan with Team Guam at the 2004 Athens Games.

In some ways it reminded me of my first years as a wrestler. I wanted to win so I could gain favor, to win so people would like and respect me, but the truth was the adult me had far more in common with the runner than my childhood self. In the years that followed the end of my career there had been times when I had feared failure. I had enough of that bitter taste of defeat and I didn't want any more of it. So, for a while at least, I held back. I avoided risking too much and stayed away from the potential of defeat. I did enough to get by. I went for a jog instead of going out for a sprint.

But there were other things about her that made me think. I saw her react in a way that so many others

– including myself – react. When hard truths are shared we often shrink from them, refusing to listen. So many times in my own life I wanted to run from the hard things – the challenge, the criticism, the call to push harder and dig deeper. In those moments we stop seeing the coach as someone who wants the best for us, and instead see them as an opponent. And that rarely works out well.

Not all the lessons I learned in Athens involved hardship and pain. I made a point of taking my athletes with me at mealtimes and sitting with teams from other countries. In this way we found out what life was like for the Iraqi soccer team and how a sixteen year old gymnast from Baton Rouge had prepared to win two silvers and one gold. But my favorite dining companions were the Kenyan runners.

In fact, there were four of them from Kenya, but one guy had not made the cut so he was in Athens running for Qatar. They told me how they were all from the same village and asked me to come and watch them as they competed in the steeplechase.

It never struck me until I was in the stadium that the steeplechase is a perfect metaphor for life. Throughout the race there are immovable hurdles that don't give way easily when you knock into them; they're tough and painful and will knock you down if you collide with them. It's a long race, not a sprint, and there are water traps and crowds and awkward twists to navigate. And as I watched those four guys from the same village run the race with purpose, running it to win but also running it as a team, I saw on the jumbotron a perfect illustration of how to get through life's challenges:

Men's 3000m. Steeplechase. Olympic Games 2004

1. Ezekiel Kemboi	KENYA	8: 05.81
2. Brimin Kipruto	KENYA	8: 06.11
3. Paul Kipsiele Koech	KENYA	8: 06.64
4. Musa Amer	QATAR	8: 07.18

The three Kenyans finished first, with the guy running for Qatar coming in fourth, exactly as the trials had predicted. It was a beautiful thing to watch, but more than the medals, it was their attitude that impressed me. That's the race I want to be able to run, I thought as I watched the four of them celebrate together. I want to grab my friends, my family, and anyone else who needs it and say, "Let's finish strong together."

Of all the memories from that summer in Greece, the one that remains the most magical comes from the wrestling venue. It happened after the Kenyans had shown me what true community looks like and after the other runners had reminded me of the perils of holding back or dropping out. I was thinking about it all as I sat in the wrestling venue some days later. Joe had come out with some guys he was coaching, and as he and I sat next to John and Ben Peterson, cheering on the wrestlers we knew from the USOTC, something inside me started to glow, like the embers from last night's bonfire as they make contact with fresh wind and new kindling. Here we were, fulfilling the very dream that Dad had nurtured within us at an early age. Our classmates laughed at our dream, but here we were, the Russell brothers in Athens, not competing, but loving every minute of it.

I was thinking how glad I was that I had not given up the race just because I had missed out on winning. I was thinking about how glad I was that even though Joe and I had both lost a dream, we had both also seen it fulfilled in unique ways. Even though the two brothers we sat next to had a combined haul of two golds and two silvers, Joe and I both knew that in life we race to finish, not necessarily to win.

Sitting with my brother and my friends John and Ben, in the birthplace of the Olympics, watching men we knew and had journeyed with as they wrestled for glory in front of us – it was the sweetest moment of my wrestling career. This was the complete fulfillment of my Olympic dream. A dream that was birthed in 1976 was finally being realized in 2004, in Athens, Greece. Sitting just behind us was Alexander Karelin, the greatest Greco-Roman wrestler of all time. The toughest wrestlers on the entire planet gathered in one place, united around the same cause of cheering others on to greatness. For years I had assumed the Olympic dream was about my own medals. At last I saw it was about so much more than that.

Years on, I still recall my experiences in Athens. I still see people who stop the race and choose to sit on the curb, condemning themselves for not being able to win. I see people who hold back and choose to perform within their capabilities in the hope that somehow they

will be congratulated for simply taking part. Then I see
those who run to win, who are grabbing their friends
and community and running with others.

My dad taught me so much. Some of those lessons I
had to unlearn, but so many of them I appreciate more
and more as life goes on. He taught me that failure is
nothing to be scared of. He taught me that to dream
is to picture the farthest possible reality – not fantasy – and to commit to reach it through a series of
small steps and measurable goals. He taught me that
to tell others what you're dreaming of isn't as foolish
as people might think, and that to experience doubt
or ridicule is not as toxic as we might fear. Most of all
though, he taught me that every experience on this
side of eternity offers us an opportunity to discover
something on the far side of life. Nothing is wasted.
Everything can be redeemed. No journey need be in
vain.

At times I thought that my journey was only going
to come into focus once it had taken me away from
my childhood. I thought that success could only come
once there had been a grand finale on top of a podium,
with a medal and an anthem and the sense of pride that
came with it all. But today I know the truth. Today I am
a pastor in a small community. I coach wrestling at the
local high school. In many ways my life is a carbon copy
of my dad's. I know that my journey has brought me
right back to where I began, but this time with me in
the role my father took on so well: encouraging, inspiring, calling people on to live boldly. For me, this is what
it means to finish strong.

My dad taught me to get back up after you fall down. This lesson wasn't just delivered in wrestling rooms and at tournaments; I saw him enact it as he got back up after he fell. And I watched my brother get back up after he fell too. And my mom. Together they showed me that life is not about the gold medals or the public affirmation. Life is about finishing strong today, whatever that may bring. It means letting go of the past and having open hands for the future – not grasping tight for fear of losing hold of success.

The truth that I have come to realize is that I am my dad. I am the son of my father. And I am proud to be walking in his shoes. I am thankful he let me into his journey, that he let me see him walk through his wilderness as he showed me how to trust his coach Jesus to lead him through.

There's no wilderness so barren that God can't get us out of it. Whether it was Joe's accident, Dad's affair or even my grandpa's lifetime of drinking; even he – aged 74 – turned his life around. After my dad prayed with him, Grandpa turned from being a drunk who smoked a couple packs of cigarettes a day into a non-smoking tea drinker that rarely missed a Sunday morning service. The community woke up and took notice, thinking if Al Russell could be saved, why not them? As a result, church attendance grew in that little town. Grandpa finally was able to tell my dad that he loved him and even though he had never seen my dad compete in a sport, Grandpa was there for my final tournament. He saw me sail through the air off the stage. He saw my Olympic dream come to an end right there and then.

I wonder if he knew that it was just the beginning of something, a new chapter that was going to be written by a wiser author than myself. I like to think that he did.

Dan and Rick Russell. Father and son running the race of life together.

HOW DO YOU FINISH STRONG?

It's 3:36 a.m. but it's warm here in the hotel lobby. And it's loud too, with the noise of taxi drivers arguing happily outside. This is Turkey and while I'm not looking forward to the eighteen hour journey home, I'm excited about getting back to Joy and our four wonderful children.

I've been away for eight days with the US Wrestling Team. We've had a good world cup championship, beating Russia but losing to Ukraine in the finals. We wrestle to win, we expected to win, but we fell short in the finals. Still, for a team like ours with the wrestlers we have, silver's a good and fair result.

I'm sitting with the coaches, medics, and wrestlers, all of us slumped over the too-small armchairs that are dotted about the lobby. In the middle of us is our haul of bags, a man-made mountain of luggage full of kit and clothes. I remember how it was always the same when I wrestled overseas, how life would slow to a snail's pace whenever we arrived at or left an airport or hotel.

Next to me is Joe Warren, one of our wrestlers and a world champion. He's fought well these last few days, especially when he faced down the local favorite with the roar of the crowd against him while the announcer gave his pre-match speech. Yet Warren stayed present, he embraced the fight, and he didn't lose a match all tournament. Next year's Olympics in Beijing should be a lot of fun for him.

I remember when I was a year out from the Olympics, both of them. I was so sure of what lay ahead, and so surprised when it turned out that the future wasn't going to be what I had dreamed of. I think, perhaps, that the shock of seeing those plans change in a single throw troubled me more than I admitted at the time. It's hard to lose a life-long aspiration in a split second; suddenly nothing makes sense any more. North isn't where it always used to be.

"Dan," says a voice by my side. I'm lost in sleep-deprived thought so it takes a second time before I register that I need to respond. "Dan," says Joe Warren, "can I ask you a question?"

"Sure," I say.

"How did you finish strong?"

"What?"

"How did you get through your career and find life on the other side of it?"

"Wow. That is a good question," I say. It's so honest and sincere and I know I'm going to struggle to articulate my reply in a way that I really need to. I pause a while and think.

I remember all those times when I really didn't finish strong at all. I think about how I wanted nothing to do with wrestling in the days after losing to Matt Lindland. I remember the way I felt as I boarded the plane in Albany, New York and sat myself down next to Cordy, my head and heart a riot of anger and sorrow. I remember staring at the trophies in my empty flat in Portland, hearing the words "this is it" change from a cry of triumph into an expression of futility. I think about weeping over bags of moldy food, feeling like an outcast at school, and wanting so, so bad to give up when Uncle Jeff told me I was no good at all. Name a year and I think I could provide a hundred different examples of finishing anything but strong.

But something in me recognizes Warren's words. Something in me knows that while I'm not finished yet, I'm still going. Am I going strong? Yes, I think I am. I'm not sitting by the curb and I'm not holding back in the hope of avoiding failure. I'm still present, still embracing what life places in front of me. I'm still saying "yes".

I wonder why Warren asked me this question. Could it be because he's at one of the places I've been in my life? Is he staring at a wall full of trophies and wondering what's the point of them all?

"Do you know my brother?" I ask.

"Sure."

"Whenever I think about what it means to finish strong I think about him. You know he was probably one of the greatest wrestlers this country's ever seen, don't you?" Warren nods. "And you know that after his accident he wanted to wrestle again. Did you know he had to crawl like a little baby to be able to learn to walk?"

"No, I didn't."

"He'd missed a year of school so he had to repeat his senior year. He went out for the wrestling team but he couldn't make the starting lineup. So, he wrestled junior varsity all year. And you know what his record was at the end of it?"

"No," says Warren, faintly.

"0 and 7. A lot of people said it was really sad. Joe said, 'If I could wrestle in high school, I bet I could wrestle in college.' So he called up a coach he knew, the top guy at University of Minnesota. The coach said, 'We'd love to have you but you'll never compete for us.' Joe never missed a practice in four years. His junior year the coach gave up and said, 'Joe, I'm going to let you wrestle in some tournaments.' Joe wrestled in two and his

record was 0 and 4. He didn't win a match."

"His senior year, the coach let him compete in four of the home meets in front of the crowd of thousands of people. In four matches Joe's record was 0 and 4 again. And again a lot of people said, that's really sad. Do you know what Joe said?"

Warren looks back at me.

"He said, 'There are far more good things that happened than bad. In fact the accident was one of the greatest things that ever happened to me. In the midst of that accident I found the presence of God. And there's joy in the midst of the suffering. There's joy in the pain.' Warren, my brother has coached NCAA champions, world medalists, and Olympic champions, but the most important thing in his life is knowing that God's present with him. That's what it means to finish strong."

Joe Russell was inducted into the Wrestling Hall of Fame.

The silence that settles on us blocks out the noise from the taxi drivers and the hotel staff busying about the lobby.

"Warren, all those trophies you've won will either end up gathering dust on a shelf or gathering dust in a box in your garage. We might think when we start out that we're wrestling so we can win medals, but somewhere along the way the guys that finish strong are the ones who realize they don't do any of this for the accolades."

"What do we do it for, then?" Joe Warren says.

"We do it for something bigger than us. We do it because it is in embracing all that life has to throw at us that we learn the truth of what life is really about. We do it because there's a God who loves us and who one day we will stand before. To those who have persevered, not given up, who have looked for His guidance and followed His voice, He will say, 'You finished well.' That's why we wrestle – with everything in life."

It's time to board the bus and make our way to the airport. Warren and I end up not sitting together and all through the journey I'm wondering about the other things I could have said; how being a wrestler today is so important because it goes against the culture that says feelings dictate everything in life. I wonder whether I should have talked about how finishing strong is about not allowing ourselves to make decisions based on emotions. I wonder if I should have reminded him the best wrestlers in the world are the ones who know that feelings don't matter as much as we say they do.

Mostly, I think about the earliest story of wrestling

I've ever read. It's in the Bible and it describes the scene when Jacob wrestles God all night long. God could have ended it at any time, but He didn't. Why? Because God wants us to wrestle with Him. Life is full of struggle. To finish strong is to embrace that struggle. To finish strong is to say yes to the fight. To finish strong is to know that all of this life here on earth is to be followed by something greater. We're here to live and learn, to wrestle and to dream. We're not here for the trophies or the finish line or the chance to look down and say we've beaten others. We're here because this life only has one final bell. And that's the only finish that matters.

I held the Olympic torch once. It was in 1996 while I was training at the USOTC. We were just two months away from the start of the Games in Atlanta and the torch was snaking its way around the country. As an athlete preparing for the Games I was invited to help carry the torch, and I will never forget the moment that it was placed in my hand.

This was before I lost to Matt Lindland, before my body took one beating too many. I was optimistic, excited, and captivated with the cast iron belief that I was on a mission that would lead me all the way to the Olympic finals. So as my fingers wrapped around the wooden handle, and my ears were filled with the sound of the stirring music being played throughout the USOTC, I got goosebumps all over. The torch had already been in the hands of pretty special people, and there would be even more to come. Even though I only held on and ran with it for a short way, I was glad I had been able to carry it toward its final destination.

We all get to carry God's eternal flame. Life itself is a beautiful demonstration of God's love and care for us, and as we live we have the opportunity to hold the flame high and proud. Each of us has been made with care, each of us created with unique potential. And just like relay runners we can only move ahead because of who has run before us. The greats of the Christian faith – Abraham, Moses, Joshua, Esther, Mary, and Stephen – have all gone before us. We live in part because of their faith and trust in God.

The buzz of carrying the Olympic torch – just like the thrill of standing on the podium at the end of the Poddubny, knowing I was the unofficial champion of the world – was a great buzz. But the next day, the goosebumps were gone. The thrill was starting to fade.

The destination to which we are heading will not be like that. Heaven will not fade, nor will the thrill of being there. But until that day, we have a battle to fight and a torch to carry.

And so I leave you with this thought. One day we will all stand before the Father. What will we see when we look back on the journey we have taken to get there? Will we know whose help and support has allowed us to grow? And who will we have passed our torch on to?

Who will we have inspired? Who will we have supported and cheered as they took their small steps forward?

For those who finish strong – who have stayed present, who have given everything, who have not merely hidden from the hard things or continually given in to the temptation to drop out when life has threatened to overwhelm us – we will see God's banner raised above us. And though we might then feel as though the finish is behind us, a whole new journey will open up before us.

ACKNOWLEDGMENTS

For Ryan, Sarah, Dani, and Hannah,

This book is for you. I have lived a full life filled with struggles and successes. The choices and decisions I have made all have played a part in your journey. As you turn the pages of this book, you will discover pieces of your own journey through my story. There are more than possessions that a father passes to his children; sin is one of them. You will read of my rebellion. You will see where my heart was hard and calloused. You will read of decisions I am ashamed I willfully chose. But sin does not have to define you, as you will see.

This year, I found a moment to hand each of you a rock with the word "LEGACY" engraved on it. I am passing on to the four of you the blessing of finishing strong. This legacy is a decision that only you can choose, but it is my biggest hope and prayer for each of you.

Finish strong and meet me at the finish line.

Dad

Ryan Jeffryes Russell

When you were in kindergarten I took you to the gym to compete in your first wrestling tournament. It was a local tournament. I was so proud to see you in your wrestling gear. The gym was packed with other parents there to support their young athletes. As we walked through the gym, I could hear people commenting, "Here comes Dan Russell with his boy. I wonder if he will turn out like his dad."

Ryan, you carried my build – long and lanky with knobby knees and elbows. I always got comments on how much the two of us look alike. I always loved hearing this observation.

I had you warm up. The match was set. We talked through a couple of moves. You stepped out onto the mat. I could feel my heart thumping. You shook hands and the whistle blew. Your opponent charged at you with great aggression. You were clearly overmatched. You lost the match, took home the silver medal that day. I had suffered many losses in my career and knew this is part of the tough journey in life.

As I walked out of the gym, I heard a dad say, "My boy beat Dan Russell's son." I realized in that moment that you would be wrestling not just an opponent, but also your dad's history. I did not want that for you. Ryan, I knew you were a smart boy and you could be a champion in anything you would set your mind too. But I determined that day that wrestling would not be your path. You would find your own course. You would learn the lessons wrestling had taught me in other ways. Ryan, whether you wrestled or not, life is a fight. You have the mind and heart of a warrior. I am proud of you. You were named after my Uncle Jeff. He had tormented me in my younger years and I wanted more than anything to see that relationship restored. You are God's gift to me of restoration.

Ryan, follow in your father's footsteps in the areas of life that are most important. Fight the good fight! Finish strong.

Sarah Joy Russell

Sarah, at eight years old you walked on the stage and sang in front of thousands. The purity and the innocence of your voice and the courage to be vulnerable in front of so many touched this dad's heart. You took the risk. There is an exquisite beauty when you are willing to be woundable. Sarah, life will try to choke out your innocence, purity, and wound-ability. You will be challenged to live life safe. There are two things I was robbed of early in life: innocence and intimacy. Sarah, I see in you the promise of those things restored in me.

You carry your mother's name. Joy is discovered in the journey. Joy comes from knowing you are loved, and that nothing in this world can take that love away.

There is joy even in the midst of disappointment and trouble, when you know a reality greater than yourself. Joy comes from a hope beyond your current circumstances. Find joy, even in the midst of crushed dreams, knowing that God has the final word. Joy is not an escape from pain. True joy enables you to face reality head on.

Finish strong with a joy that is beyond this world.

Danielle Shannon Russell

Before I met your mother, I dreamed of naming a daughter after me. The moment I first held you, I knew you would carry my name.

I remember the day you and I were walking to our car. You were very little. I was experiencing the joy of this time with you. The sun was shining and I was over-come with the specialness of the moment. You held my hand as we walked through the field toward the park-ing lot.

We were laughing, skipping, and enjoying the moment. I looked at your face with your eyes lit up and a smile that exposed the dimples on your cheeks. It was a moment when being a dad brought incredible joy.

The laughter continued as we got to the big parking lot. I remember the instant you saw our car in the park-ing lot. You got so excited. Your passion is contagious. As soon as you saw the car, you let go of my hand and started running toward it.

It all happened so fast, but I remember the next minute as if it were a slideshow in my mind: a red sports car rounding the corner at a high speed, my voice erupting with a shout of panic and desperation, the screech of tires and the nearness of death.

You did not see the car barreling toward you as your eyes were fixed on the parked car. This is where you are most like your father. So many times in my life the destination was more important than the journey. This led to poor decisions and great pain. Finishing strong is not about the destination but the journey. Your Father in heaven delights in you. Enjoy His presence as He enjoys you. Hold His hand and He will get you to the finish line safely.

Dani, your beauty and brilliance light up a room. You have certainly brought joy into my life. You journeyed with me in the writing of this book, inviting your friends Desi and Ruby into the journey as well. I have been grateful for these times. I have watched you sit with others in their pain in a way that has given them strength. You are the kind of friend that few are lucky to have walk beside them. I have watched you battle through tough obstacles. It is in the overcoming that you have something to offer others in the heat of their own battle. Run the race to win. Finish strong!

Hannah Noel Russell

Early in your life hidden things were revealed to you, even in your mother's womb. You have felt pain and injustice from your first days. You have chosen to stand next to others as they have walked through tough times. Your grandmother wrote a book titled "It's Time," from a dream you had at 5 years of age. She tells the story of your dream in the chapter titled "Season of Grace".

Hannah, your name means favor and grace. There were many years of my life when I believed favor and grace were nowhere to be found. I struggled with feelings of being unwanted and unloved. You are a stunning reminder to me of both favor and grace. Through you, I have understood myself in deeper ways. Thank you.

You have many gifts that your mother has passed on to you. You look so much like her, and remind me of the grace and favor I have found with her. For many years, your mother has helped me wrestle through the lies I chose to believe. I see you walking with others as they are faced with crippling lies. I see you leading them into the truth.

Sometimes life just doesn't seem fair. Dreamers can be faced with unfairness and injustice. But when we are convinced that life isn't fair, it's time to trust in God. You can know that God is working all things together for the good, even when life takes an unexpected course.

God may lead us into difficult places, but He has a plan for us there. Listen, God is speaking tenderly to you. Hear His voice because He is helping you to finish strong. He has great strategies for you. He intends for you to flourish.

We have had deep, profound conversations through